LIFTING EVERY VOICE

LIFTING EVERY VOICE

*My Journey from Segregated Roanoke
to the Corridors of Power*

WILLIAM B. ROBERTSON

WITH BECKY HATCHER CRABTREE

FOREWORD BY GOVERNOR LINWOOD HOLTON

UNIVERSITY OF VIRGINIA PRESS

Charlottesville and London

University of Virginia Press
© 2022 by the Rector and Visitors of the University of Virginia
All rights reserved
Printed in the United States of America on acid-free paper

First published 2022

9 8 7 6 5 4 3 2 1

Library of Congress Cataloging-in-Publication Data

Names: Robertson, William B., 1933–2021, author. | Crabtree, Becky, author. | Holton,
    A. Linwood (Abner Linwood), writer of foreword.
Title: Lifting every voice : my journey from segregated Roanoke to the corridors of
    power / William B. Robertson with Becky Hatcher Crabtree ; foreword by Governor
    Linwood Holton.
Description: Charlottesville : University of Virginia Press, 2022. | Includes
    bibliographical references and index.
Identifiers: LCCN 2021035779 (print) | LCCN 2021035780 (ebook) |
    ISBN 9780813947174 (hardcover) | ISBN 9780813947181 (ebook)
Subjects: LCSH: Robertson, William B., 1933–2021. | Holton, A. Linwood (Abner
    Linwood), 1923- –Friends and associates. | Virginia. Governor's Office—
    Employees—Biography. | Peace Corps Kenya—Biography. | African American men—
    Biography. | African American educators—Biography.
Classification: LCC E185.97.R615 A3 2022 (print) | LCC E185.97.R615 (ebook) |
    DDC 975.5/044092 [B]—dc23
LC record available at https://lccn.loc.gov/2021035779
LC ebook record available at https://lccn.loc.gov/2021035780

Cover photo: William B. Robertson on the steps of the Virginia State Capitol Building,
1971. (William B. Robertson Papers, Archives Collection, Bluefield State College)

For my children and grandchildren,
Bernice Victoria Robertson,
William Allen Robertson,
Eva Marie Robertson,
and
Teddy Robertson,
the joys of my life,
and
America,
my country,
the country I love so very much

Whenever I hear songs such as "The Star-Spangled Banner" and "America the Beautiful" or recite the Pledge of Allegiance, I get teary-eyed. These are symbols of what we want America to be. However, we must realize that as a nation, we have not achieved true equality for all our citizens. Recognizing our shortfall, let's do something revolutionary. Let us join Colin Kaepernick and take a knee. Then, as one America, patriots all, let us rise and go to work eradicating bigotry, hatred and prejudice in our land. Let us unite America. To do less is simply ignoring reality.

—William B. Robertson, *Baltimore Sun*, September 7, 2017

CONTENTS

FOREWORD

On the evening of May 30, 1973, in my last year as governor of Virginia, my twelve-year-old son, Woody, parked his bike behind the governor's mansion and ran up the ornate early nineteenth-century staircase to deliver startling news. While delivering Richmond's evening newspaper—one in which I was regularly lambasted for my progressive views, especially on race relations—he had been attacked by several boys his age. They wanted money and he had none, so they gave him a few smacks before he could make it into an apartment building.

The boys, who were African American, lived in a poor neighborhood just off Woody's paper route a few miles from Capitol Square. Although unhurt, he was rattled—and worried that they would come after him again, or perhaps accost one of the area's numerous elderly residents. As governor I had unique recourse: several undercover police officers accompanied Woody on his rounds the next day. His assailants came after him again, took marked bills, and were detained and cited before being released to their parents.

But the cops were not the only ones who accompanied Woody that day. I had asked my special assistant for minority and consumer affairs, a former elementary school principal named Bill Robertson, to find out about these young men. As they were arrested, he was standing on the curb across the street, pretending to read a newspaper but actually observing closely. He followed up by visiting their homes, where he discovered the absolute squalor in which they and their families were forced to live.

When Bill reported back to me, he made the kind of proposal that showed what kind of person he was. Given these young men's circumstances, he said, our duty was not to punish them but to give them the opportunity to come by some spending money by honest means. The result, as Bill describes in chapter 15 below, was "Operation Self-Help." He invited Richmond business leaders to a luncheon where he and Woody persuaded them to donate to a summer jobs program for about one hundred underprivileged kids. Looking back from the perspective of half a century, I wish we had paid them more for the hard work they did, mostly cleaning up vacant lots, but they did get an opportunity they had not had before, and they owed it all to Bill Robertson. Newspapers all over the United States and Canada reported the story, focusing on Woody's role in helping raise the funds. As was typical of Bill Robertson, he kept in the shadows, taking no credit for the project he had conceived and carried out.

As you will read in *Lifting Every Voice,* Operation Self-Help was only one of the many creative ways that Bill found to help others. As the first African American to serve in a professional capacity in the Virginia governor's office, he faced an uphill battle every day, but he accomplished a great deal, with his two most powerful weapons being persistence and charm. The most important of his many successes came in knocking down barriers to African Americans seeking employment, both with private businesses and with the Commonwealth of Virginia. When he and I took office, not one of Virginia's one thousand state troopers was African American—and the superintendent was in no hurry to make a change. But Bill stayed after him, and eventually the force was desegregated. He worked his magic in countless other agencies as well.

In December 1972, barely a year after the famous Attica prison riot in upstate New York, inmates in the Virginia State Penitentiary also took over part of their institution. Bill rushed to the scene and took the lead in negotiating a peaceful resolution. As you will read in chapter 14, he listened to the prisoners' grievances—they really were enduring terrible conditions—and also the concerns of the overworked and underpaid guards. Bill tells you how he resolved the situation, but let me contrast his compassionate approach to that of my friend and fellow Republican Nelson Rockefeller, the governor of New York. In the Attica riot, thirty-three prisoners and ten corrections officers lost their lives. At the Virginia penitentiary, the death toll was zero.

When I brought Robertson to Richmond, he was already well known throughout our state—and among Jaycees nationwide—as the founder of Camp Virginia Jaycee, which served disabled kids. And his service continued for decades after my term as governor. He became the head of the Peace Corps for Kenya and later deputy assistant secretary of state for African affairs. His boss for much of that period was Ronald Reagan. Bill never had any illusions about President Reagan, but he was the type of person who could get along with anyone who would enable him to serve others.

Robertson's service continued to the end, into his ninth decade. In Baltimore, where he spent most of the year recently, he became a tireless advocate for the "squeegee kids," who earn money at stoplights by cleaning motorists' windshields. He recognized that they are just trying to earn an honest living, making them not so different from the Operation Self-Help kids.

I knew Bill for more than fifty years, yet I learned an immense amount from *Lifting Every Voice*. It is, to begin with, the extraordinary story of his growing up under segregation in the southwestern Virginia city of Roanoke, where my wife, Jinks, and I were raising our own children. Jinks and I both hailed from families that were able to send us to expensive colleges, and I found that what my city and state offered me was only as limited as my ambitions. But Bill saw his own father become increasingly embittered as more and more less-qualified White men were promoted over him. One of the Holton family's favorite treats was visiting Roanoke's amusement park, Lakeside, which for years barred its gates to black families like the Robertsons, as Bill's family painfully recalls.

Years later, Bill and I discovered that we had known each other longer than either of us had realized. During my years as an attorney in Roanoke, my offices were in the Shenandoah Building in downtown Roanoke. Sometimes I would stop to chat with one of the cleaners, who often brought her son to work with her. That turned out to have been Bill and his mother, Rebecca Robertson.

As you read this book, you will no doubt be as heartbroken as I was to learn what my friend had to go through growing up African American in the *Green Book* South. But I suspect that even more, you will be moved by Bill's fighting spirit. Early in life, he committed himself to fighting injustice, which of course meant constantly witnessing it up close and personal. But he decided that whatever he experienced, he would remain an optimist. He kept to that decision for more than eighty years.

As I initially wrote this in June 2020, many White Americans were belatedly discovering just how much more privilege and opportunity they have had than their African American brothers and sisters. For many Black participants in movements like Black Lives Matters, it has to be exasperating to see White folks take so long to learn so little, and I can certainly see why many give way to despair. I respect the pessimists; God knows the facts often seem to be on their side. But if I know anything about Bill, it is that his optimism, sometimes justified and sometimes maybe not, was his great strength.

You will read a host of amazing stories in *Lifting Every Voice*, but I think the book and Bill Robertson are both summed up in a single snapshot he provides from one of his countless visits to Camp Virginia Jaycee: he witnessed a blind camper pushing a paraplegic friend's wheelchair, with the rider providing directions. A sad sight? Not to Bill. For him it was one more proof of how far we can go together.

LINWOOD HOLTON
Governor of Virginia, 1970–74

ACKNOWLEDGMENTS

We wish to express heartfelt gratitude to our family members who have supported us and given us time to follow this dream, especially our extraordinary spouses, Ruth and Roger, who carried on without us and silently brought us plates of food when we were so immersed in this book that we didn't take time to eat. We honor the persistence of Victoria Robertson, who would not let her father rest until he wrote down his story, a process that took more than forty years. We publicly thank the dozens of role models who guided us by word and deed during our lifetimes and those who educated us, our teachers, most especially those at Bluefield State College. We wrote this book in humble recognition of those who came before, on whose shoulders we stand.

Our book would not have been possible without a complex network of people and events. The generosity of Linwood and Woody Holton, standing as a testament of friendship over the years, sped our work on its way. Librarians and officials at Bluefield State College, James Leedy, Jim Nelson, and Nancy Adam-Turner, endured our questions and opened their doors for us to research and marvel at the school and its past. The dedicated librarians in the Virginia Room of the Roanoke City Library searched newspaper files with heaters at their feet in the cold. Nadine Zimmerli and the staff at the University of Virginia Press have been so very kind and patient with us as we learned the behind-the-scenes tasks of book publishing. Our countless friends, near and far, have contributed words and photos and made this book better. Special thanks are due to those who took the time to read and edit and make suggestions: Thelma Daley, sixteenth National President of Delta Sigma Theta Sorority; Sonja Garcia, fourteenth South Atlantic Regional Director and Chairman of the International Archives Committee at Alpha

Kappa Alpha Sorority, Inc.; Tracy Hale Clark, sixty-fifth State President of the Virginia Jaycees; and Bill's brothers in the Knights of Peter Claver in Tampa and Baltimore. We also appreciate the hospitality of the De Cheke family in Baltimore for providing us a comfortable place to talk and write. We are grateful for the peoples of the world, especially in the sixty-five countries served by Bill Robertson who taught him that humans are the same around the globe and that fathers and mothers worldwide want to make a living and hope their children can be safe, educated, and successful. The knowledge that we are part of the same humanity strengthens us all.

In addition, our work has been touched by the meticulous editing of Fran Allred and Mickey Johnson at We Edit Books, the ever-encouraging, knowledgeable Connie Taylor at Fathom Publishing Company, the wordsmithing skill of Lauren Trovato, and the magic of photographic artist Jacques Polomé at Jacques Polomé Design.

Finally, we recognize that behind all these gifts of love and friendship and skill is the Giver, the good Lord above. We give thanks to Him for smiling on our efforts.

These words, ordered and readied in the spring of 2020, were subject to the drastic lifestyle changes wrought by the COVID-19 pandemic. Instead of being defined by this plague and the nationwide racial injustice such as that recently occurring in Minnesota, we must continue to come together, to become and remain brothers and sisters and conquer the cruelties of the world with our strength of unity.

Publisher's note: William Bernard Robertson passed away on June 22, 2021, at the age of eighty-eight, while his book was in production. Although he saw his memoir through to its almost final form, we regret that he did not live to hold a copy of the bound book itself. We express our deep sadness at the loss of this extraordinary man. We also express our gratitude to Becky Hatcher Crabtree and Victoria Robertson for their dedication in seeing this book through to publication. May William B. Robertson's story inspire us to ensure that every voice can be lifted to rejoice in equal liberty.

LIFTING EVERY VOICE

INTRODUCTION

My journey to "be somebody" started many years ago and took many paths. I well remember Mrs. Mattie Morris, my first-grade teacher at Gainsboro School, a segregated public school in Roanoke, Virginia, introducing "Lift Every Voice and Sing" to my classmates and me. It is a beautiful and powerful song that has served me well throughout the years.

My ancestors talk to me via the song. They provide guidance, direction, and inspiration. They highlight the fact that I should be proud of who I am and glory in what has been achieved by those who were kidnapped, stolen from their homes in Africa, and impressed into America's evil, billion-dollar-plus institution of slavery. They and their descendants endured slavery, Jim Crow laws, and segregation, yet with God's help, we played a major role in building this country. Through the lyrics of this song, we send a message to the foes of African Americans—raise your voices and sing this song together as American brothers and sisters. Join with us and sing together. Change is coming. It is inevitable. Either join our "march to victory" and let liberty and equality prevail or get out of the way.

There have been many significant stops along the way. One of the most consequential was the place I found myself on a steamy August morning in my eighty-sixth year. It was difficult for me to comprehend that day in 2019 that I was to be honored by the renaming of the library at Bluefield State College, a historically Black college, the school where I matriculated, matured, graduated, and learned to become a professional.

As I looked over the audience, I felt the electricity in the room. It was like a Sunday church service. The crowd was made up of well-dressed, finely groomed men in suits and shiny dress shoes, and fashionable women in high heels and a variety of dress styles and flowing pantsuits. They relaxed in the air-conditioned facility after finding their way around the terraced hills of Bluefield State and climbing up the slope in the heat to the library. Friends from long ago greeted one another and renewed the bonds of shared memories. Photographers kneeled before the podium with the long lenses of their digital cameras pointed at the speakers, poised to get the best shots in the crowded room.

I gripped the lectern, a comfortable position for me after a lifetime of public speaking, and began to speak as seventy years of my life unfolded before me. The parade of memories included the day I realized I didn't have enough money to register for college; my efforts to earn two degrees; the conferring upon me of an honorary degree; and my association with five United States presidents, who sent me to sixty-five countries to represent the American people.

Men and women gathered in the library punctuated my short speech with applause and cheered me on with cries of "Oh, yes" and "Praise God" as I spoke of the virtues of libraries, but especially this one, rich with history. I saw the smiles, and mine matched theirs. To be in this place, this important place, now with my name on the door, was a joyful and gratifying experience.

This was happening to me, a man born and raised in segregated Roanoke, Virginia. I realized how good God had been to me. This special moment caused me to love and appreciate even more Bluefield State College, the life I had lived, and the country I had served.

Other important moments cascaded through my mind, clear as day. All of them changed my life and rerouted my destiny. Woven like a shimmering golden thread through the fabric of my life was divine intervention. Whether it was my first days of college; the kitchen of my childhood home with Mamma; dancing the night away with my wife at an awards presentation dinner; selling apple jelly; negotiating in the midst of a prison riot; acting on behalf of the governor of Virginia in a prison hostage situation; working from a variety of offices in Washington, D.C.; organizing volunteers in Nairobi, Kenya; planning my beloved Camp Virginia Jaycee; helping dismantle apartheid; or changing attitudes worldwide, I had also been changed. So many places and people had altered my path, but I was drawn to the place where I stood that day, the college whose library now bore my name.

Indeed, it was validation that I had become somebody.

1

EARLY DAYS

I was seventeen in 1950 on a hot August day when my father and I walked to the train station near our home in Roanoke for me to board the Powhatan Arrow, a sleek Norfolk & Western passenger train. I was on my way to southern West Virginia to enroll at Bluefield State College (BSC). My dad worked for the railroad so I had a free pass to ride the train. The rest of my life teetered precariously on the outcome of this trip.

I was excited but managed to listen to his last-minute advice: "You will only need three shirts, one on your back, one in the drawer, and one at the cleaners." He told me that there were going to be students there who possessed more than I. "Money and clothes are not important," he said. "Your focus must be on doing well and graduating." My father had shown us all our lives that our attending college meant everything to him. He had gone to college, too, but he was from a family of twelve, and when he and Mamma married, he dropped out. He wanted his children to be part of the American dream of middle-class status and values, and he felt that education was the path to that dream.

There were a few other African Americans in the segregated train car. I swallowed the feeling of anxiety and pressed my forehead to the window to watch cornfields and the often-unseen back doors and backyards of little towns speed by. When I was calmer, I recalled an incident from years before when, early on a Sunday morning, I was delivering newspapers in Roanoke. I watched a busload of young men unload at a service station to get sodas and snacks. They looked like giants to me. I found out they were members of the Bluefield State College football team heading home after a 55–0 rout of St. Paul's College in Lawrenceville, Virginia, the previous day. I thought I might want to go to Bluefield State. Now that had become a real possibility. My parents and I considered Negro colleges in North Carolina and in Virginia's Tidewater area, which was not favorable for my asthmatic condition. I could not enter White institutions such as Virginia Polytechnic Institute (now Virginia Tech), the University of Virginia, Roanoke College, and others because it was the era of segregation. The healthier choice was to go northwest to the mountains of West Virginia.

When the train stopped in Bluefield, I moved quickly to get off and begin this new chapter of my life. Alone, I found my way through town to the school and climbed the steps to the administration building to register for classes. I had never been to Bluefield before, but I knew that it was smaller than Roanoke. The mountain air there was crisp and fresh, but there was a hint of coal dust near the train yard. Those train tracks went right down the middle of town, and there were mountains on both sides. In those long-ago days, huge lighted signs advertising "Sunbeam" and "JFG" glowed from the top of the mountain along with a clock, the hands visible from a mile or so below. The houses perched on the side of the mountain were new to me, too. I had never imagined houses in such steep surroundings.

My observations that first day were overpowered by my emotions. I was excited. My mind raced with the realization that the plan for my life was on track. "I am finally here," I thought. "I am at college. This is a red-letter day in my life. I am here." These feelings made the next event of the day so hard.

After going through the registration process, I realized that I didn't have enough money. It was as if I had the wind knocked out of me. I called my father and told him. College for me and for my seven brothers and sisters was his dream; he had talked about it as long as I could remember. I knew he was bitterly disappointed, and so was I. "There is no more money," he said bluntly. "Get the next train and come on home. We can check on some of those schools in North Carolina later. Maybe we can afford them."

I was in front of Conley Hall, looking down the street, cardboard suitcase in hand, about to walk or maybe hitchhike to the Bluefield train station, when the longest car I ever saw stopped in the street, and the driver, a portly man, motioned me over. "Where are you bound, young man?" he asked.

"The train station," I told him. "Can I get a ride?" He introduced himself as Dr. H. L. Dickason, president of Bluefield State College, and told me to get in. So, I did.

He drove about thirty yards to a driveway and pulled in. He asked me several questions and found out my situation. He scribbled out a note. "You go to the dining hall, tell them I sent you, and show them this note," he said. "Get a good meal, then get a room at the dormitory, Payne Hall, and get a good night's sleep. Report to my office at 9:00 a.m. tomorrow."

I did exactly as I was told. The next morning, I was at his office at 8:30. This very kind, soft-spoken man authorized payment of what I had on hand, made arrangements for me to register, found me a job, and let me make monthly payments on my school fees. When I look back on my life, I see that moment as providential. The intensity of my desire to go to college made Dr. Dickason's help so much more important. I felt the hand of the Lord in his actions that day. If I had gone home, I would never have gone to college, and my life certainly would not have been the same.

Bluefield State College was a teacher-training institution. There were seven hundred students when I enrolled. The campus was unique, not flat like those of many colleges, but built on terraced hills. I fell in love with the college grounds, and they became even more beautiful to me as I began my studies there.

I had really wanted to go into law, but I understood there was not enough money for that extended education. History and social studies were as close as I could get, and they became my majors. I credit my seventh-grade teacher, Mrs. Madge J. Wheaton, for making history come alive for me. The study of English fascinated me, and so English became my minor. The spoken word drew my attention like a magnet. I even enjoyed diagramming sentences to better learn the structure of communication. The choice of education as a career gave me the opportunity to influence countless students. I was content with my choices.

Right off the bat, the school let me know that I had value. This kindness and concern that Dr. Dickason showed me on that first day was evident in all my professors. They taught me that the sky was the limit. I had a professor, Othello Maria Harris-Jefferson, who said: "Let no mountain stop you. You go around it, you go over it, or you go through it." She taught me how to teach in her "Methods in Teaching" class. She also supervised my student teaching. Her mantra: "I don't care where you go; I am preparing you to teach anywhere." She and I were especially close; she was my instructor, my mentor, and my friend. We discussed everything: BSC, and local, national, and international issues. We did not always agree. She dropped a young man from student teaching because she felt he was not ready. I disagreed and recruited others in the class to go on strike. That happened on a Friday. By Monday, other students had chickened out, and so I joined them and went to class. She found out about the failed rebellion and called me aside. "Mr. Robertson," she said, "do you think I wouldn't have failed every one of you?" Years later, after the young man had retaken the class and become a successful teacher, he confided in me: "She was right. I wasn't ready then."

"In all my years of teaching," Professor Harris-Jefferson told me, "I have taught eight outstanding students, and you are one of them." Her opinion of me strengthened my commitment to always do my best. When I faced problems long after my time in college was over, I would drive back to Bluefield and find inspiration walking the campus and then talking my concerns over with my mentor. I relied on her often, and she came to rely on me. Professor Harris-Jefferson proved her trust in me when she confided that her brilliant sister had been traumatized by a violent personal attack. She asked me to care for her sister if she departed the Earth first, leaving her sister alone. I willingly accepted that trust. In her later years, I visited my professor in the Beckley hospital. Then, when the time came, I handled the arrangements for both her sister and her after their deaths.

Other professors emphasized the need to prepare ourselves for the new day that was coming. They espoused the belief that America could not continue down the road it was traveling: equity was coming. Opportunities would expand for African Americans, and my teachers wanted us to be prepared. All felt that the future would be better. Without a textbook, Professor John R. Rankin made history, geography, and government come alive in his lectures. Professor W. E. Hebert, an art instructor, showed me that art and life mirror one another. BSC president Stephen J. Wright, who followed Dickason, and everyone else on staff did not give up on me and did not let me give up on myself.

At Bluefield State, I learned to debate, to separate fact from propaganda, to teach, and to write. I learned to listen and to respect the opinions of others. I loved the classroom as I did the dances, sports events, and Greek life. Perhaps the most important thing I learned is that if you keep your head and heart in the right places, anything is possible in America. That is what America is supposed to be about. I wanted to make a contribution to the country that I loved, and I believed that America would meet me halfway on that two-way street. Black Americans had loved and been faithful to America, and we would someday be treated as first-class citizens. I loved the philosophy of Bluefield State College.

However, the latter part of 1950, near the end of my first semester in college, was a disappointing time for me. The young lady I hoped would be my wife turned me down that Christmas. I was home for the holidays and had proposed marriage on the condition that we delay the wedding until I completed college some three and a half years later. Ruth Price was pretty and smart and athletic, and we had been friends since our early years at Lucy Addison High, when she moved to Roanoke. We began to date in our junior year in high school, and I escorted her to the senior prom. My heart was broken.

Like many college freshmen away from home for the first time, I was lonesome. For the first time in my life, there was no one to wake me up. My schedule called for three classes on Monday, Wednesday, and Friday and two classes on Tuesday and Thursday. I thought there would be more free time, and there was not. Finances were always a problem. Also, I lived with the knowledge that the fees I needed for college were taking money away from home.

There were times that I wanted—no, needed—to go home to Roanoke, especially during my freshman and sophomore years. The Greyhound bus ride home, round trip, cost $6.50, and I knew if I could come up with $3.25 to get home, I could get some help at home to pay the remaining $3.25 to return to Bluefield State. The bus left at 8:30 p.m. and arrived in Roanoke three hours later. My younger brothers and sister were in bed by that hour, and my father was at work, but my mother would get up and let me in. One night when I arrived she started pulling ingredients from the shelves and baked a chocolate cake, my favorite, in the middle of the night. We sat up until dawn, talking and eating warm chocolate cake. In my mother's kitchen I was surrounded and strengthened by her love.

I did not do my best work the first three years of college. My grades were good enough to get me by, but not by much. The Almighty must have recognized that I needed something else to stabilize and fortify me. Working through Bluefield State, he sent Johnnie Early to me. Johnnie was also a student when she came into my life, a beautiful, intelligent young lady who changed my attitude and constantly made my heart throb. I remember walking in the rain with her without realizing it was raining, and the warm spring afternoons we spent just talking about the future. "You are bright," she reminded me over and over. "You are special. You can do great things." This was my junior year, and she was a freshman. She became my best friend, my motivation, and my inspiration.

I was initiated in 1953 by Omega Psi Phi, the first international fraternity founded on the campus of a historically Black college, Howard University, in 1911. I was given a pin, the symbol of pride in this organization that lifted the ideals of "manhood, scholarship, perseverance, and uplift." There were three Omega Psi Phi brothers engaged to be married at that time. I remember that we three shared an engagement party given by our fraternity.

If an African American man went to college from Roanoke, most came back Omega men; some were Kappas or Alphas. I enjoyed the organization, its ideals and the songs. Professional men joined it. My membership put me in the same league as doctors and lawyers and teachers nationwide. This practice was also part of the college experience of Black women. They joined similar academic, social, and service sororities such as Alpha Kappa Alpha and Delta Sigma Theta that provided strong lifetime support for professionals.

In November, Johnnie and I were married. We were young and in love. We knew our families would tell us, in the words of Nat King Cole's hit, you're "too young, too young to really be in love," but we were convinced "we were not too young at all."

I had no doubt that marriage was the right thing to do, based on love, not on necessity. How wonderful was this feeling—this thing called love. For the first time in a long time, I was back on the right track. Things would be better because I would make them better. I was going to be a teacher, and I would be the best teacher ever. Johnnie was responsible for this newfound confidence.

I took Johnnie home for Thanksgiving to introduce her to my family. Except for Mamma, who knew our secret, everyone present thought she was my girlfriend—that is, until I announced at Thanksgiving dinner that we were married. My father's immediate and irreversible response was that he was finished supporting me. He wanted me to return home after graduation and help send the next child to college. That was a common practice in large families, but it would not happen with me. I knew, without question, that I had to assume total responsibility for myself and my new wife.

On Monday, I was back in Bluefield, looking for a job. Divine forces were at work again. As I entered the door of the Moose Club to find work, a big man, the manager, Carl Porterfield, came out the door looking for a worker. I worked there the rest of my college career. The Porterfields helped us. They raised a large garden, and I will never forget the baskets of produce they provided for our young family.

I was a senior in college when the U.S. Supreme Court ended public school segregation on May 17, 1954. My professors at Bluefield State taught me to prepare myself for an integrated world. Those men and women instilled in me a great sense of service. Martin Luther King Jr. and others started to open doors, and because I had stood on the shoulders of giants like Dickason, I was prepared to enter those portals. I earned two bachelor's degrees at Bluefield State College, one, in 1954, in secondary education, social studies, and English, and another, in 1956, in elementary education.

These successes, educational and otherwise, were built on the foundation of my childhood. During my early years, I didn't consider my perspective as a Black child, my opportunities for learning, and the constant exposure to getting along with others in a family and a community to be important, but they were vital to the life I have lived.

2

CHILDHOOD

Mastering Home, School, and Community Climate

I was born to Irvin and Rebecca Robertson in Roanoke, Virginia, on January 21, 1933, at the height of the Great Depression, and christened William Bernard Robertson. I was the first son of what was to be a family of eight children—six boys and two girls: Faye, William Bernard, Stanley, Patrick, Barry, Jackie, Ellen Marie, and Vincent.

Our home at 419 Fifth Street probably looked as if it needed to be torn down, but looks were deceiving because it held lots of love and happiness. My neighborhood was in Northwest Roanoke, once a White residential area. By the time I was a child, the White people had moved farther west in Roanoke, and it had become a Black community with a diversified population in terms of occupations and ages. Professionals—doctors, lawyers, and teachers—lived there along with cooks and waiters who worked for the railroad, good jobs at the time, as well as laborers. The residences were of varying quality, some larger and more beautiful than others, but in Roanoke we were all limited by race to this area. All age groups were represented—young families, children, single people, and senior citizens. We prefaced the first names of the older people with a respectful "Uncle" or "Aunt." Everyone knew everyone else, and all raised the children and took responsibility for them. The values of the neighborhood were shared, and a community priority was to guide all the children to success.

Our living room was inviting: clean and neat and brightened with slip-covers hand-made by my mother. I remember a big Philco floor-model radio that I curled up beside and called out answers to Groucho Marx's quiz show. We had books and magazines and newspapers available in the living room, where we spent hours reading. There was a cook stove in the kitchen that required wood and coal for heat, so there was a trace of smoke associated with home and happiness. The upstairs held two bedrooms, one for our parents and one for the children, only three of us at the time. Later, we separated the room by hanging a sheet to divide the space and give my older sister, Faye, some privacy.

Our parents expected us to be inside by 3:00 p.m., the time Dad got up to prepare for his night shift. He was a laborer for Railway Express Company. He helped unload trains, a job requiring heavy lifting of packages and other items, and he worked the nighttime hours. The night air contributed to his difficulties in breathing, as did his habit of smoking, and eventually to the emphysema that would take his life. We always ate dinner together as a family. He talked about work, and we reported on school and the news of the day. Like most children during those days, we bathed on Saturday nights. Mamma heated water on the stove and poured it into a tub on the kitchen floor. Faye bathed first and then me, then Stanley. The kitchen was warm and cozy, the air scented with the clean-smelling lather of the floating bar of Ivory soap. Meantime, while we bathed, Mamma squeezed the bubble of orange coloring that came with the white margarine. This distributed the color so the margarine looked more yellow, more like butter. We were all ready for another week.

We had an extended family surrounding us: grandmothers, grandfathers, and cousins. There were aunts and uncles who were blood relatives and those who were not but nonetheless had as much influence on my life as those who were related. Respected neighbors helped raise us as much as those connected by family ties.

My mother's parents, Mary and William Roberts, were beloved. They had a car and visited often, bringing cakes and pies. When my mother's father died, her mother, my grandmother, didn't like being alone and would bribe us to spend the night with her. We were glad to go. She bought us sodas and generally spoiled us. We knew when she told us to "Be a man," she meant to be like her husband, our Papa.

My father's parents did not visit as often. William Robertson, my father's father, died before I was born. His wife, Nora, my paternal grandmother, was born just a few years after slavery ended and lived to be nearly one hundred. She raised turkeys and chickens, and Grandma always provided us with a big Thanksgiving turkey. We didn't feel as close to her as to my mother's mother. She did not care for my mother and resented that my father had married her and that she had absorbed the financial resources of her son. That side of the family exhibited high tempers; my uncles and father were often angry. Systemic racism, which created dead-end jobs with no opportunities for advancement, seeped into the core of strong men and women and reemerged as discontent, dissatisfaction, frustration, and, sometimes, violence.

As a young child, I do not remember life as being difficult. I remember having plenty to eat. Mamma cooked lots of beans, chicken, cabbage, potatoes, tomatoes, and often pies and cakes. She tried to make everyone's favorites. Mine was chocolate cake, but if another child wanted apple pie, she made that, too. Also, we dressed adequately. My mother always smiled and stood tall. She was a college tennis player in Petersburg, Virginia, before she met my father, a seminary student in college at Lynchburg.

My mother was a beautiful, loving person. She taught me manners and how to use words like "please" and "thank you." She talked to me about how to treat women and just how to be a good person. I thought my mother was the most beautiful woman in the world. As a young child, I spent a lot of time with her. I went with her as she visited homes to measure and deliver chair covers. Her profession was creating custom slipcovers. She always talked to me, inspiring me. While I was a child, she read the classics to me, *Little Women, Gulliver's Travels,* and many others. If she saw an article in a newspaper that she felt I should read, especially those about the Black congressmen Adam Clayton Powell (a Democrat from New York) and William Dawson (a Democrat from Chicago), she pointed them out. We would discuss the piece after I read it. Mamma was connected to the PTA and visited school often. I was always proud when she came to school. She was beautiful, inside and out. As a teenager, I referred to her as my best girlfriend and said I would marry her if she were not my mother. She didn't talk about troubles with my father, but she said enough that I knew she wasn't happy, and I knew from an early age that I must protect her. I dearly loved her. I can never adequately explain what she meant to me because she meant everything.

As I sit quietly now, I can almost hear her voice talking about nothing and everything. "Do the very best you can," she often reminded me. The smell of starch brings back the fragrance of her neatly ironed white blouses and aprons and just takes my breath away, memories of her are so strong.

When I was a child and I went to town with my father, he put on his Sunday clothes and had me dress in the same way. The Black district was in the Henry Street–Gainsboro area with hotels, restaurants, theaters, the library, churches, drugstores, the newspaper building, YMCA, YWCA, clubs, insurance companies, and ice cream parlors. There was something going on seven days a week, twenty-four hours a day. After church on Sunday, I would take Ruth to a theater and then for ice cream. Members of the Black population went to Henry Street for some reason or another two or three times a week. After so-called integration, this area of Roanoke deteriorated. Recognizing the social and economic value of Henry Street, members of the African American population are now trying to revive it.

"Town" was the bigger business district on Jefferson Street and Campbell Avenue. We liked to go to town, which was crowded and a lot of fun. It was one of our only opportunities to see White people, plus we always got a treat, cookies or a cake, and the purpose of the trip was usually to purchase something new, such as shoes or an item of clothing. The hustle and bustle of crowded streets and stores was exciting.

Dad maintained that dressing up to go to town reduced the racial put-downs by White store personnel. It showed he meant business. He tipped his hat to Black ladies in town and waved at Black men. He explained to me that the problems of segregation were the same for everyone in the Black community and we all experienced it. Greeting each other, he felt, helped lighten the load for each of us. All members of the Black community faced common problems, and most went to some church. Sunday services, they felt, provided the opportunity to "refuel" spiritually in order to get through another week of dealing with White people.

Roanoke was divided into four sections, Northwest, Northeast, Southwest, and Southeast. African Americans lived in three of the four sections; there were no Black people living in Southeast at this time. Black residents took tremendous pride in their neighborhoods, and they would confront Black people from other sections and harass them verbally as they walked through. It was more talk than anything; we called it "woofing." When I walked from my home in Northwest to visit my girlfriend in Northeast during high school, I would hear calls, "Here comes a Northwest boy," or "What are you doing here, Northwest?" This was a call to others to come out and confront me. I remember hearing a young male voice shout, "Oh, leave him be, he's just going to see Ruth." I passed on by without confrontation.

As I got to fifth grade, my teachers sent me to town with money to pay their bills: the light bill, water bill, and phone bill. Many Black teachers could not afford cars, but they had me, and I was happy to run their errands. Mamma had always been afraid for me to go to town so I didn't tell her I was going regularly for my teachers. When she found out, she spoke proudly, "That Bernard has been going to town all this time for his teachers!" She marveled that I was trusted with the cash and the responsibility.

My father was a highly intelligent, proud man. He loved us, worked every day, and taught me how to make a living and be responsible. Like other Black men, he worked hard for less to provide for his family. It was hard to be a man with the weight of the world, including Jim Crowism and segregation, on his back. The periods of being knocked down and having to continually get back up were brutal. If things had been different, he would have had no limits, he could have been anything; he had the skills to have been an excellent politician. I am so thankful for the sacrifices he made and the values he instilled in me to improve my life. Both my parents worked hard and showed us love.

Christmas was a time of special happiness and celebration. We always had a Christmas tree, family was nearby, and there was an abundance of good food and gifts. One year, Faye found the toys beforehand and showed them to me. The realization that the gifts were already in our home destroyed my magical childhood beliefs but also strengthened my appreciation and admiration for our parents. Dad worked six nights a week and was off only on Sunday. On Christmas mornings, he would come home at about 1:30 a.m., wake us up, and watch us open gifts, then go back to work and return about 7:00 a.m. and expect oysters for Christmas breakfast. His usual routine was to sleep until 3:00 p.m. and go back to work at 11:00 p.m.

In our segregated world, little contact was made with Whites. The insurance man would come by. We saw Whites downtown. My father worked on the railroad, and we often traveled to Newport News to see my mother's cousins. When traveling by train in the South, African Americans were limited to the first car behind the engine—the "colored," or Jim Crow, car. Mamma always packed a lunch for the trip because we were not allowed to eat in the dining car. People would share with each other, get to know one another. The colored car was a buffet of delicious odors with one member of each family clutching a shoe box of homemade fried chicken, sandwiches, potato salad, boiled eggs, and other foods. We loved the window seats and watched the world fly by outside as the clackety-clack of the train lulled us to sleep. My father's railroad pass also allowed us to journey to New York to see other relatives. The segregated car was used as far as Washington, and then, I always thought, Whites joined us. In reality, the Norfolk & Western Railway portion of the trip was segregated, but when we changed trains to the Pennsylvanian on the way to New York, we sat wherever we wanted; the cars were not segregated. That's the way it was all over Virginia at that time. Once we left Virginia, traveling west, even at Bluefield, just over the Virginia state line, the trains were nonsegregated and we could move around. Traveling east, we were not allowed out of the colored car.

Imagine being a parent and having your child ask, "Why do I have to get in this car?" or "Why can't we eat in the dining car?" or "Why can't we sleep in the sleeper car?" How could parents answer? They didn't like it, but they had reached the point of angry acceptance, and then had to pass that feeling on to their children, that they were somehow less than those who could ride on other train cars and were powerless to change the situation.

Little did I realize then how this bigger system of segregation affected our father, family, and me. Over the years, he literally became a tyrant because of his inability to progress in his job. He worked for the Railway Express Company, affiliated with the railroad. Even though he had two years of college, he was never able to advance because of his color. On the day he left, because of disability, he was doing the very same thing that he had done the first day, thirty-six years earlier. Yet, he had trained many young Whites who had just come out of high school. As these young Whites rose in the organization, they became his superiors. His immediate superior was a very nice man who came to our house on Christmas Eve and brought oranges and tangerines, part of the old paternalistic system with the mind-set that Whites must take care of Blacks. As I grew older, I realized this was not what my father needed. He needed a promotion so he could buy his own oranges and tangerines.

My daddy learned quickly; he could have done any job that the company asked of him, but he was not given the opportunity. The use of "boy" when addressing Black men and "girl" when addressing Black women was demoralizing. The idea then that Blacks were childlike and needed to be taken care of affected family life because Black men and women were not given the opportunity to reach their potential. Indignation, anger, and frustration followed, especially for men like my father. Frustration internalized for years without release added to out-of-control tempers and even violence for many Black men and women.

Both my father and mother attended college, but left to marry. My father was enterprising and had a number of businesses of his own in addition to his railroad job. He knew how to make money and was always busy. His endeavors included time as a promoter holding dances in Leo Hall in Northwest Roanoke, operating a nightclub, the 308 Club, in the Black community, and bringing some of the top entertainment acts to Roanoke, such as the Mills Brothers and the Ink Spots. He and Mamma were excellent ballroom dancers and enjoyed this activity very much, but the nightclub business fell off in the late 1930s, when nightclub competition forced small operations out of business.

During childhood, my time, energy, and interest were consumed by school, selling papers, and World War II. I started school in 1939 at age six and really liked it. I learned to read quickly. My home was always filled with reading materials—classics like *The Adventures of Tom Sawyer* and *The Adventures of Huckleberry Finn,* for example, and comic books, daily papers, and magazines.

I attended public schools staffed by Negro teachers. Of the thirty or so public schools in Roanoke at the time, only four were for Black students. There were three high schools: two were for White students and the other was for Black students. The Black schools were certainly inferior in many ways, but the teachers were part of the extended family. They taught not only subject matter but also racial pride and the concept that things would always get better. Their repeated admonitions still ring in my head: "You have to be able to compete." "You have to be on time." "You have to be a better person . . . better employee . . . better leader." "You need to know these things for the future."

My schools observed Negro History Week, now known as Black History Month. The concept originated with Dr. Carter G. Woodson in 1926. Woodson, recognized as the father of Black history, was born on December 19, 1875, in New Canton, Virginia. His parents had been slaves. He worked in the coal mines of West Virginia. Carter graduated from Douglas High School in Huntington, West Virginia. He graduated from Berea College in Kentucky and was the second African American to receive a Ph.D. from Harvard University. W. E. B. Du Bois was the first.

In 1925, Dr. Woodson founded the Association for the Study of African American Life and History (ASALH). My wife and I are currently proud members of this organization. As snowbirds, we belong to both the Baltimore and the Tampa chapters. There are ASALH chapters in cities throughout the country. Woodson wanted America to know that Black Americans had made and continued to make tremendous contributions to the country that treated them as second-class citizens. He wanted America to know how much Black lives mattered. In 1926, he started Negro History Week in February of each year. In 1976, under President Gerald Ford, it became Black History Month. It was a special time when Black teachers and students and all Americans celebrated the contributions African Americans had made to America. During my time in the segregated Black schools in Roanoke, we studied the contributions of Black citizens year-round, not only during Negro History Week.

Black students sang with great pride "Lift Every Voice and Sing," the Black National Anthem. We opened devotions with "The Star-Spangled Banner," pledged to the flag, and closed devotions with "Lift Every Voice," written by James Weldon Johnson, which expressed faith, hope, and belief in victory in overcoming the chains of slavery, and proclaimed love of country. The first time I heard it, I recognized the beauty and power the words contain:

Lift every voice and sing
Till earth and heaven ring,
Ring with the harmonies of Liberty;
Let our rejoicing rise
High as the listening skies,
Let it resound loud as the rolling sea.
Sing a song full of the faith that the dark past has taught us,

Sing a song full of the hope that the present has brought us.
Facing the rising sun of our new day begun,
Let us march on till victory is won.

It is a song of survival. White Americans need to sing it, too. It ought to be about lifting our voices together and about integration becoming the equal sharing of the positives of all races. My heart adds to the lyrics, "We have survived! I am not inferior! Recognize my worth!"

3

WORLD WAR II

In the summer of 1941, at age eight, to earn change for movies and other things I wanted and did not want to bother my parents for, I began to sell the *Norfolk Journal and Guide,* a Negro newspaper, one of the top publications in the country. It sold for ten cents, and I received three cents for each paper sold, usually selling ten each week. This meant I was making thirty cents per week. A soda only cost five cents, a Baby Ruth candy bar cost five cents, movies were ten cents, and a bag of popcorn was five cents. This meant that I had a nickel left over for Sunday school.

The *Norfolk Journal and Guide* was a very good paper, well written by quality reporters. It carried news of the Commonwealth, nation, world, sports, and local news of Norfolk and Portsmouth. I began to learn more about my home state by reading the paper I sold as well as improving reading skills, increasing my knowledge of world and U.S. geography and history. I also learned how the larger society dismissed and paid little attention to contributions by Black Americans.

On December 7, 1941, "a date which will live in infamy," Pearl Harbor was attacked. Faye and I had gone ahead to Sunday school, as usual, and Mamma and Dad came later with the younger kids. We had just returned from church and were preparing for dinner when we heard the news via radio. I could tell this was really important by the way the announcers spoke. We really did not know where Pearl Harbor was, but we knew it was an American base. The local paper put out an "extra" that day. I wish I had kept a copy.

The papers were filled with news of the war, which dictated everything. Rationing was the order of the day for sugar, meat, gas, and some articles of clothing. I remember my mother coming to school to obtain rationing stamps. Students observed air raid drills by closing shades and getting under desks. Air raid drills were observed at night with shades down and lights off, and air raid wardens were assigned to neighborhoods to see that rules and regulations were followed. Teachers taught us the geography and history of the war. We were excited to hear and learn about the American industry turning from peacetime to wartime—how we transitioned automobile plants from cars to tank production, for instance. Each Saturday as I went to the movies, I bought a war stamp for ten cents to go in a book that could be turned in for a war bond when it reached $18.75. There was such a great sense of working together, of patriotism, to defeat a common enemy.

The White press did not report the military contributions made by the Negro outfits, the Ninety-Second and Ninety-Third Infantry Divisions and the Ninety-Ninth Fighter Squadron, which was also known as the Ninety-Ninth Pursuit Squadron and the Tuskegee Airmen. Black women also served as WAVES, WACS, and nurses. The WAVES were slow to accept Black women, but they eventually did. However, accounts were carried in the Negro press. Parents, wives, sweethearts, and friends bought the papers to keep up with the exploits of their sons and husbands overseas. They also sent these papers to the men in the war areas and military bases across the country in order for them to know what was going on back home. The *Journal and Guide* told us of Dorie Miller, a Black seaman who worked in the galley of his ship at Pearl Harbor and came up on deck to shoot down an enemy plane and save his captain. I was so proud of those who looked like me. This should have been hailed by all Americans, Black and White, but that was not the case. We had a few White customers, wives of White officers connected with these groups. They, too, were locked into this system of not being able to read in the White press what the units were doing.

My father and brother joined me in selling newspapers after Pearl Harbor. For the next five years this was a lucrative business. We went from selling 10 to 1,500 papers per week. We began, in addition to the *Journal and Guide,* to sell the *Baltimore Afro-American* and seven other Black publications: the *Pittsburgh Courier,* the *Chicago Defender,* the *New York Amsterdam News, Ebony, Jet,* the *Roanoke Tribune,* and the *Charleston Color.* I read each of these nine different papers thoroughly. I knew of every lynching, every shooting, every Black leader and sailor, soldier, and Marine who made the news and how they were treated after the war. Each paper tended to be the same in national and international reporting, but each was different in its state and local sections. Our weekly earnings were in the neighborhood of forty-five to fifty dollars. This was good money in those days and really helped supplement my father's railroad pay. My father worked at Railway Express by night and sold papers during the day. It became basically full-time for my father, brother Stanley, and me.

Newspaper sales began to decline when the war ended in 1945. However, segregation and discrimination heightened. There was a sense on the part of those of us of color that the war, which brought about a closer relationship between the races as we fought a common foe, would continue and grow, but it did not. Black veterans expected more.

About this time, I was in fourth grade at Gainsboro School. The teachers there were excellent. I knew many of them from Sunday school and even had an aunt who taught there. However, a problem arose. I became the target of older boys, bullies repeating fourth grade, who wanted me to do their schoolwork. My grades plummeted, and my teachers and parents recognized that something was troubling me. I was placed in Harrison School for summer classes, and I flourished. The decision was made to leave me there for the regular term, and I remained there through my seventh-grade year before going to Lucy Addison High School in eighth grade.

Selling Black newspapers helped lay the foundation for my life. They taught me how to read, about Black history, how to meet people, how to count money, and how to make change. The papers exposed me to a larger world. Not only did I vicariously grow up in the Pacific and in Europe as I followed the coverage of the war, but the *Afro-American* newspaper actually sent me to New York City. Because paper sales had begun to decline when the war ended in 1945, this paper sponsored a contest to increase circulation. My brother Stanley and I both participated. In 1946, in the summer between my seventh and eighth grades, we won a three-day trip to New York City. Some 115 *Afro-American* newspaper carriers from Maryland, Virginia, North Carolina, and South Carolina earned a train trip to New York City, and we were among them. We rode the subways, took a sightseeing trip around Manhattan Island on a yacht, visited the Bronx Zoo, the NBC studios, Radio City Music Hall, and Coney Island. My favorite was watching the Brooklyn Dodgers play baseball against the St. Louis Cardinals at Ebbets Field in Brooklyn. I pulled for the Dodgers because Jackie Robinson was playing in their farm league program. The weather was perfect all three days. We stayed in the Salvation Army Men's Club on 124th Street, where we were required to write and send cards and letters home. It gave me a whole new perspective on the world. I never forgot that trip and what it did for me.

Newspaper sales diminished to the point that we got out of that business and went into the huckster business, selling oranges, apples, bananas, meats, greens, and such from an open-panel truck. Dad got off work at 7:00 a.m., but he didn't drive, so the driver picked up Dad at Railway Express, went to the market to replenish the vegetables, and took me to school. I rode in the back with a stick before school started and after school was out and hit those who tried to take an apple or an orange without paying.

My family had outgrown the little house on Fifth Street. My parents bought a house, and we moved to the 800 block of Loudon Avenue just across the street from Loudon Elementary School. When we went out our front door, we could see very little except Loudon Elementary School, which was so large that it blocked the view of the next street. I was too old for elementary school by then, but I had brothers who could have been students there. It was a school for White children only, thus my brothers could not go. We couldn't shoot basketball or play on the playground even during after-school hours without being called names and dodging rocks thrown at us. I was a docile little boy, and I didn't fight, but I felt it. We felt it. Anger. But what does anger get you?

4

JACKIE ROBINSON AND
MY DREAMS

It was about this time that Jackie Robinson broke into the major leagues with the Brooklyn Dodgers. I had followed him closely when he played at Montreal the year before, more so than my other hero, Joe Louis, the boxer, who had been the idol of the Negro community for so many years. I loved baseball and the legendary players such as Josh Gibson and Cool "Papa" Bell who never made it to the majors because of a strict segregation system. But my hero was number 42, Jackie Robinson, the first African American to play modern-day Major League Baseball. He opened the 1947 season as a first baseman for the Brooklyn Dodgers on April 15.

For the first time my friends and I saw someone who looked like us hit the ball and run the bases as a member of a major league team. Indeed, we all wanted to be like Jackie. He taught us so very much—not to give up in spite of adversity and hostility. Jackie was subjected to racial taunts, slurs, and beanballs. He was deliberately spiked, could not eat with the team or stay in the same hotel in certain cities because of the color of his skin.

Jackie led the Dodgers to the National League pennant. He led the league in stolen bases, batted just below .300, and was named Rookie of the Year.

My ambition at the age of thirteen was to take his place when he retired, because I loved baseball. I wanted to be a major league player. Yes, we all wanted to be like Jackie, but not all of us possessed his athletic skills. While I did not have his ability to play the game, I gained so much more from him: his quest for education, his lessons of perseverance, pride, and confidence in self, and his modeling of effort to make positive contributions to society. Also, he exemplified the fortitude to never quit on the ballfield or in life. Upon retiring after ten years of brilliant play, Robinson was elected to the Baseball Hall of Fame as soon as he was eligible. Not only did he change baseball, Jackie Robinson changed America. Those who remember still celebrate Jackie Robinson Day on April 15. I never dreamed that day of remembrance would be observed more than seventy years later, when, on the anniversary of the day he started professional play, the major leaguers and the nation saluted our hero by having all ball players wear Jackie's retired number 42.

To illustrate how much we thought of Jackie Robinson, when our mother was expecting a baby in April 1947, Stanley and I were determined that, if the baby was a boy, he would be named Jackie Robertson, almost Jackie Robinson in our minds. Our little brother was born on April 19, 1947. Our parents had other names ready, but we persuaded Mamma and Daddy to add Jackie to his name, and he became Jackie Frank Lewis Robertson.

5

HIGH SCHOOL DAYS

Trials and Triumphs

As a teenager, the institutions that most shaped my life were family, church, and school. My family had grown larger in the late 1940s and made my father more frustrated because his pay had not grown. It is hard to explain what a segregated system can do to the mentality of a proud and intelligent man or woman who is locked into a system from which he or she cannot escape. Home became the place I did not want to be. Forsaking baseball and the things one generally does at home, I began to work at hotels and other businesses in order to earn money for clothes, school, and other needs, but most of all to stay away from my father, who, because he could not rule on his job, became a virtual dictator at home. As time went on, he became more and more angry, and when his children got in trouble, he was often furious. He wanted so badly to become more important and for us to reach the goals he envisioned for us that anything less was unbearable. He became physically abusive to my brothers and sisters and even to my mother. Perhaps through divine intervention, I chose to walk away during tense times that seemed to be escalating and did not engage in those heated confrontations. Mamma and I spent a great deal of time together, especially once my father became so tyrannical.

I knew about the Black colleges in each state in the country because I read the Negro newspapers. My mother had attended Virginia State College in Petersburg, and my father had attended Virginia Seminary in Lynchburg. My father constantly said he did not want me to be in the position he had found himself in for so many years, and that I must finish whatever I started, especially school.

My father's family had belonged to the Mt. Zion African Methodist Episcopal (AME) Church for generations. My mother was Baptist but had joined the AME Church so that we could worship as a family. Our teachers at school were the Sunday school teachers at our church. We took part in plays and programs at church for Easter and Christmas. I learned public speaking at AME Church programs. The people of the church supported me and made me want to make them proud.

I also remember, as an eighth-grader at Lucy Addison High School, the quiz program put on by the seniors of the school. Two opposing teams were asked questions by a moderator, who then threw them to the audience if no one answered. As an eighth-grader, I was way up in the balcony with my homeroom class. The question came to the audience: "What are the three Negro divisions in the armed forces?" My hand shot up, and I was able to answer correctly to the applause of the student body. Another question: "Where is the Notre Dame Cathedral?" Again, my hand shot up, and again I responded correctly, "Paris, France," to the roar of the student body. My teachers and peers congratulated me during the course of the day. I was able to answer because I read. I was an avid reader whose reading materials included those Negro papers. I fell in love with American history and government at an early age. Negro History Week played a major role in this love affair, but also Mrs. Madge J. Wheaton, my seventh-grade teacher, just set me on fire in this arena. She made classes so interesting.

I graduated from Lucy Addison High School in Roanoke, as did several of my siblings. It was the sole all-Black high school in Roanoke before integration. Some alumni say that Lucy Addison provided higher-quality education than many White schools in the South. I was remembered in the senior superlatives of the Class of '50 as "Most Humorous" and for being mischievous and loving to have fun. In the class prophecy, my classmates playfully predicted I would be a prominent Philadelphia attorney. I have fond memories of Addison and those classmates and teachers who impacted my life.

Our class poem, particularly the last two verses, summed up the way many of us felt as we graduated during such a time of change to face the unknown:

Farewell, dear teachers, you've
Served well, not only lessons
Taught, but you have fought with us the fight
And given us the strength to do what's right.

In our onward struggle upward
As through life we all must go,
May your guiding spirit follow
Through a world we do not know.
—Azalia Reynolds, Class of '50

6

COLLEGE AND BEYOND

No one seemed happier than my dad when I graduated from college. He attended the ceremony with Mamma and several of my brothers and celebrated in the gym following the formalities. Mamma and he danced as others crowded around them to watch. He revived the old tradition of throwing money to the band, and others joined him.

Johnnie and I had lived in a small apartment on campus. During the graduation festivities, a former roommate, Allen Mines (for whom I named my son), his mother and brother, my parents, several of my brothers, and my wife and I were all packed in the apartment visiting until it was time for the ceremony. The mother of my friend looked at him lovingly and told us all how proud she was of her son. I have since thought that this would have been the perfect time for my father to share his obvious pride. It would have been nice to hear him say it one time, but he didn't. He went so far as to say aloud, "Well, I am not proud of my son." I had supported myself and my wife, I had maintained contact with my mother and father and siblings from a distance away, and I had graduated on time. He was still angry because I had gotten married and left home. He could not soften even enough to give me a word of praise. For years, I have asked myself if he would be proud after this event or that recognition, but at that time, I bounced right back. I couldn't wait to get out into the world after college. My confidence level was so high that I felt that I could compete with anyone. With Johnnie by my side, I was off and running. I was prepared to go out and change the world.

I had earned a degree in 1954 in social studies and English and couldn't find a teaching position. I took a job at Peoples Drug Store (now CVS) in Roanoke as a custodian and delivery man. I wore a white jacket and picked cigarette butts and receipts off the floor of the store and delivered prescriptions to call-in customers. Even with a college degree, this was the best job I could find. Meanwhile, White high school students were hired and allowed to operate the cash register, but I could not.

Both of Johnnie's parents were teachers in Wyoming County, West Virginia. Her mother had difficulties with her vision and needed to retire. She called her superintendent to see if I could complete the school term if she retired. He agreed, and so my first teaching job began in January 1955. It was in a one-room school, Laurel Branch, in a "holler" just a few minutes from downtown Oceana. There were thirteen students in grades one through eight, all of them with the last name "Cook." I learned a lot there. The school had a coal stove for heat and two outhouses, one for boys and one for girls. The children's parents were farmers or had jobs in local stores. One of my fondest memories is of our outdoor physical education classes. The children were excited to go outdoors and play softball. When we went out to the field, community members joined us. I remember sixty- and seventy-year-old men playing softball with us and never missing a catch, true community interaction.

I knew the job was only for the length of the school term as schools in West Virginia were about to be integrated, so I finished there in May 1955.

I learned that there was a need for male teachers in elementary schools, so I went back to Bluefield State College for a year and earned a degree in elementary education. I took classes in music and math and did student teaching again with younger students. We then moved back to Roanoke.

Because professional people in Roanoke knew my father and me and also knew the superintendent of schools, they spoke to the superintendent about me teaching in the Black community. In an unplanned turn of events, I was offered a position at my former high school, Lucy Addison High School, in the fall of 1956. I felt immense pride in even being considered for a teaching position there.

It is hard to describe how proud I was to be hired as an instructor of English and social studies at my alma mater, a segregated Black high school. I was now part of the staff that produced me. It just could not get any better than that. I was honored to be part of this talented group of people. However, as a young teacher, I struggled with decisions regarding my students in a changing world. One event in which I was in charge of student safety scared me badly.

Of course, our southern upbringing was filled with restrictions because of contemporary segregation patterns. Inferior amenities for Blacks were common during our childhood. There were separate entrances for Black moviegoers, public water fountains separated for two races, and Blacks were required to sit in the back of the bus. Large geographic areas provided no public sleeping accommodations for Blacks, so truck drivers often had to sleep under their trucks. Because of a harsh system of segregation, Black car travelers found it necessary to have more than one driver when driving through the United States.

Hotel and eating accommodations were not available to Black Americans. Therefore, it became necessary to know where friendly accommodations were located. According to the Black historian Harry Tunnell: "The Negro Motorist Green Book popularly known as the Green Book, was a travel guide intended to help African American motorists avoid social obstacles prevalent during the period of racial segregation commonly referred to as Jim Crow." The Green Book listed businesses that would accept African American customers. I remember a scary event after which I realized that my students would have benefited from a Green Book. Before the three-hour bus trip, it never occurred to me that it would be necessary.

That year the school scheduled football games with Park Central High School in Bluefield, West Virginia: a game there in 1956 and one in Roanoke in 1957. Mrs. Hebert, a friend and teacher at Park Central High, and I decided to bring students in both directions to Bluefield and Roanoke. This was done to help ensure safety for students who wanted to attend these games.

With money students paid for the trip, I engaged a Greyhound bus with a driver to carry approximately forty students to Bluefield. We left Addison at 2:00 p.m. on a Friday with an arrival time of about 5:00 p.m. We would eat at the Greyhound terminal and then be ready for an 8:00 p.m. football game.

I failed to foresee how excited and restless a group of young students could become. They wanted to eat. "Let's stop and eat!" was the cry. I knew the area very well. I also knew prevailing attitudes of the time. I had been a regular reader of the nine Black newspapers that I sold. They all highlighted lynchings, so I understood the White-supremacist attitudes across the South. I had been refused services in Southwest Virginia based on my color. I couldn't even buy a hamburger at a local drive-in. They told me they didn't serve "coloreds." I knew the risks.

Somewhere near Pearisburg and Narrows I gave in, and we stopped at a diner. The students had money, were nicely dressed and polite. I think for a moment I forgot how racist things were. I was surprised at the welcome we received as we entered the diner. The waitresses were polite. The students purchased hot dogs, hamburgers, and drinks. Some ate in the restaurant, but most of the students carried their food to the bus. I know I heard someone on the staff say, "Stop here on your way back to Roanoke after the game."

We traveled on and attended the game and then headed back to Roanoke. I planned to travel down US 460 to home, but again the children were restless; they wanted to eat and wanted to stop at the same restaurant. They also remembered someone asking them to stop there on the way back. Things had gone so well when we stopped on the way up that I let down my guard again, and we stopped on the way home, at about 1:00 a.m.

What ensued was frightening. I really thought some of our students would get hurt or be arrested. When the students and I walked into the diner, I didn't recognize any of the staff because the shift had changed. No waitresses looked familiar, and a man, the owner, began to holler, "You can't come in here!" We attempted to explain that we had been invited back. He declared that he couldn't or wouldn't serve us. The children were getting sodas out of the box to keep them cool. The owner was hollering at us, and the students were hollering at him. What a mess! I was afraid that local and state police would come on the scene and that it would prove to be detrimental to my students. They could have gotten hurt or been arrested.

They should have been served. They were high school students with money. They were well dressed. Then I heard him say, "If the truckers on 460 hear that I'm serving colored people, I'm ruined."

At that moment, I questioned where I was. I asked myself, "Is this America? What is the problem?" The problem was that we were Black. If a White group had stopped there, the group would have been welcomed. My students had the right to request service from a business that served the general public.

With the help of my chaperones, I got the children back on the bus. The parents had trusted their children to my care. This was not the time for a sit-in or demonstration. I wanted to end this nightmare and get the children home safely to their parents.

This situation is what a *Green Book* would have helped us avoid. However, in America, there never should have been the need for a *Green Book,* and I would suggest that there is still a *Green Book* mentality in many parts of America. This has to be erased—completely done away with.

During the Depression and in the subsequent decades, Blacks still left the South for better opportunities in the urban North, but times got so hard that some opted to stay on their farms in the South, where at least they could raise their own food. Racial violence and lynching occurred. I always believed that White children grew up free, whereas Black children grew up inhibited, told to keep their hands in sight while shopping, to never touch merchandise until ready to purchase for fear of accusations of theft, and to never argue with police, just to obey them in whatever they told you to do. This was America!

7

JOHNNIE GOES BACK TO SCHOOL

After a year, the superintendent heard that I had a degree in elementary education and requested that I move to Gilmer Elementary School. I agreed and taught there for eight years. I truly loved the children, and it was somewhat nice being the only male on the faculty for most of my tenure there. The female teachers were supportive. For example, when I fixed my daughter Victoria's hair at home, they added any needed finishing touches at school.

I was considered an excellent teacher, and I coached segregated Little League baseball, football, basketball, and track. My teams won many awards for their championship play. These sports teams and the championships brought to the school endeared me to the students and their parents. In addition, the student failure and dropout rates improved during those years.

On the opening day of school in Roanoke City Schools, all the municipal teachers assembled in the gymnasium of Jefferson High School, the White high school, to be welcomed to the new school term and to be presented with the district's goals and new policies. Each school's faculty sat together. All the White schools' teachers sat alphabetically in the front of the gathering, then the Black school faculties sat behind them or in the balcony, again in alphabetical order. The point, other than to keep Black and White teachers from sitting together, was to make us feel inferior.

Later, integration came to Roanoke, and I was asked if I would volunteer to integrate the faculty at a formerly all-White school, Lee Junior High. I did so and thoroughly enjoyed teaching there. My principal, Waller Howard, was a no-nonsense White man. I remember him coming down the hallway with a child in each hand, discipline problems whom he was bringing to my classroom for help. He said he never thought White parents would call him to say they wanted their child in a class taught by a Negro, but they had. That's what Professor Harris-Jefferson and others had done for us—prepared us to function well anywhere we were. We had stood on the shoulders of giants and could do no less.

I became active in civic affairs and the father of two beautiful and healthy children. Johnnie and I welcomed Bernice Victoria, born in 1954, and William Allen in 1958. All was well with our little family of four. I had a job teaching during the school year and a job on the playgrounds during the summer.

However, there was one major problem: there was never enough money. The children were growing and needed things. Johnnie needed clothes. We needed a car and a house. There were expenses involved with my community work. Johnnie tried to help by selling Avon, but that was just not enough. She had only completed one and a half years of college. It finally hit me that Johnnie needed to go back to school to earn her degree. It would give us more money as a family and provide some security for her as well as a sense of accomplishment. She had always been told at her home in rural West Virginia that she would start things but never finished them. Therefore, as I began to talk to her about returning to college, I stressed these things: (1) If I were to die, she would be a professional woman and could be more selective about another man to marry, not just someone who wore pants, but someone more on her level; (2) it would give her a sense of accomplishment and pride; (3) it would change her image with her family: mother, father, and siblings; and (4) it would raise our standard of living.

This was a daunting task. She did not want to go and used the children as the main reason not to go. Bluefield State College was three hours away, and we did not have a car. Victoria was four and a half years old, and Allen was one and a half. I finally convinced her that I would see that the children were fine. I was counting on my mother keeping them, for a salary, of course. This was February 1960. For the next four months, Johnnie taught me how to comb, brush, and plait Victoria's hair, bathe them and lay their clothes out the night before, fix the macaroni and cheese, cook a meatloaf, prepare the roast, bake bread and cakes, and more.

In the meantime, I proposed the idea of babysitting to Mamma, who said, loudly and emphatically, "NO." I later learned this was a good decision. My father was adamantly opposed to the idea. He felt that it was Johnnie's father's responsibility to send her to school, not mine. My father was still bothered that I did not return home after college and help my siblings go to college. My efforts to convince him that we were husband and wife and needed to work together to get ahead meant nothing to him. We lived in an upstairs apartment, and the wife of the couple downstairs did not work. I asked her if she would help, and she agreed. Her only responsibility would be to look after Allen during the day.

In late August 1960, we began the greatest endeavor in which I have ever been involved. Johnnie, at twenty-six, was returning to Bluefield State College for two years and a summer. It was a day of mixed emotions for me when Johnnie left for Bluefield, even though she would return two weekends each month on the train to visit us, especially the children, and take care of tasks that I was not very good at, especially the ironing. We tried to have as much time together as a family and as a couple during the weekends when she was home, but it was difficult. The end result—her graduation—was very important to us all.

Each of us had an individual responsibility that would make this work. Johnnie would be the student. Victoria would be the lady of the house, and she and I would work together to keep Allen happy. I would attempt to hold the entire effort together.

We had a home freezer, and I tried to plan meals for a week at a time. A White lady from the grocery store would stop by and help me calculate the quantity and items I would need. We had conversations about Johnnie going to school, but the lady couldn't grasp why my wife didn't go to local colleges and stay home. Never having faced the limitations of racial segregation, she had no idea that Johnnie was not allowed to enroll in Roanoke colleges.

I remembered how my mother had sent me packages on the train from Roanoke to Bluefield when I was in school and used that idea during this time. Often, I would prepare cakes for my wife and go to the train station to give them to waiters on the train, my neighbors, and family friends. They would look for Johnnie at the Bluefield station and deliver the cakes to her.

It was a good system, one of the advantages to being a part of the Black community.

Mrs. Nadine Wheaton, daughter-in-law of Mrs. Madge Wheaton, lived across the street, and we taught at the same school. Since I did not have a car, I paid her for transportation to and from school. Her daughter was the same age as Victoria and would be attending the same nursery/kindergarten class. After I got dressed and fed Victoria and Allen in the mornings, I delivered Allen downstairs, and Victoria went with the Wheatons and me to our school.

We decided that Johnnie should live in the dorm at BSC to make certain that she would be warm, meals would be prepared for her, and, on cold snowy days, she would be right there on campus. In addition, Johnnie had support from a grandmother and several aunts in Bluefield.

Things went well for a while, with each of us going through our own agonies. The children missed their mother, and I missed my wife. At twenty-six, she was in a dorm with seventeen- and eighteen-year-olds who showed little maturity.

I soon found out that the lady who kept Allen put him back in bed soon after I left and demanded that he stay there most of the day. I had to let her go around October. Our children's maternal grandmother came and stayed until January with the same job description, but it became too much for her. She loved the children, but her sight was bad and she needed naps during the day.

Now it was up to me. I got up in the mornings, dressed, prepared breakfast, and got the children up and dressed them (which also meant doing Victoria's hair). My little girl was so much help to me, setting the table, washing the dishes, and making the beds as best she could. She was and still is the joy of my life.

I put Allen, our precious baby boy, in nursery school. My brother had a three-hour job in the evenings from 6:00 to 9:00 p.m. cleaning offices in a bank building downtown. He was going to give it up. I told him I wanted it. It paid fifteen dollars a week, and that was sixty dollars a month.

I surrendered all coaching activities and the assistant superintendent role at my Sunday school. The cleaning job at the bank required me to be there from 6:00 to 9:00 p.m. Monday through Friday and from 8:00 a.m. to noon on Sundays. Saturday was our day off. My schedule included getting ready in the morning, getting the children ready, preparing and serving breakfast, joining the lady across the street, taking her children and mine to the nursery school and kindergarten, going to school and teaching, picking the children up, changing them into play clothes, preparing dinner, walking downtown and cleaning offices, walking home, putting the children to bed, marking papers, and doing lesson plans. During the time I worked at the bank, my young sister or one of my brothers would come to babysit Victoria and Allen. I generally was in bed by 11:00 p.m. I tucked the children into their beds and would invariably awaken during the night to find one right under me on one side and the other under me on the other side. If I had turned either way, I feared I could have crushed one of them.

To ease the efforts of Johnnie to travel home and give the children a change and a surprise, I carried them to Bluefield on the train to spend time with their mother whenever I could. On Saturdays, I took them to the nearby playground to play most of the day. The time went by, and, in May 1962, the Lord blessed us with Johnnie's graduation.

God had been so good to us. There had been no major illnesses. She finished in the time we allocated. In August, she got a job teaching. We bought a car in August and a house in November of that year. Working together and with God helping and blessing us, we accomplished our goal. I was so proud of her.

During these years, my father's behavior had become more abusive, and, in 1959, after nearly thirty years of marriage, my mother divorced him. She bloomed with her new freedom, became qualified to serve as a substitute teacher, and enjoyed her work with children. If I had important decisions to make, I often consulted with my mother. We continued to have regular phone conversations. Within three years, Daddy died, unhappy and alone.

In 1963, I decided it was time for me to start working on my master's degree. I applied to Radford College and was accepted. Johnnie was up to the challenge, and I appreciated her support.

Radford was less than an hour's drive from our home in Roanoke. It had been a girls' college, the women's division of Virginia Tech, but had just recently gone coed. The graduate program had always been integrated male and female. By the time I enrolled, Radford had completely separated itself from Tech.

Initially, as I discussed my coursework, my advisor attempted to steer me to Virginia State College, a historically Black college a long way across the state from me, which meant I could only attend in the summers. He emphasized it would be easier for me—the coursework, that is.

I could drive to Radford and take courses and be home at night. I told my advisor I would attend Radford and not Virginia State College. I did this for a full year and two summers. I attended classes on Tuesday and Thursday after my teaching day was over. During the summers, I went early each weekday. I found again that Bluefield State College had prepared me well. With lots of hard work, I was able to succeed in graduate school.

I found it enjoyable being there. Although there were problems at other institutions in the South, I found none of this at Radford. I was included in everything, study groups, clubs, and all activities. People reached out and asked my opinion on this or that issue. It was an enriching, enjoyable experience.

A Black woman, Mrs. Elsie Claytor Wiggins from Roanoke, enrolled a quarter before I did. We were the only two Black students at the school. Mrs. Wiggins and I were never in the same classes. Therefore, we were able to carry the "Black experience" to White professors and fellow students who were unfamiliar with it. We shared Black history, current events, and our views of things. It was a wonderful position in which to be.

With a few exceptions, our presence was well received and looked upon as a learning experience by our classmates. Often hurtful things would be said without the intention to offend, but simply reflecting a lack of knowledge. For example, in one of my classes I scored a 98 out of 100 on an exam, and the professor said that I had set the curve so high that my classmates should take me out and lynch me, a poor choice of words. It should not have been said, but it was not said with hatred or animosity. It was new to some of these individuals that someone Black was setting the pace, and past traditions and unfounded biases kicked in.

In August 1965, Mrs. Wiggins and I became the first African Americans to graduate from Radford College, which is now Radford University. I am thrilled to be a Highlander.

8

JAYCEES AND APPLE JELLY

In 1965, I was selected by the Roanoke Jaycees as the Outstanding Young Educator in the City of Roanoke. Mr. Howard, my principal at Lee Junior High, had nominated me. He did not have to do so; it had taken a lot of nerve for him to nominate an African American teacher so soon after the integration of the schools. Years later, I learned that the judges had talked to Jaycee officials prior to announcing the winner. "The winner is a Negro. If you want us to change it, we can," the judges said.

"We want the winner," was the Jaycee representative's response.

I was invited to an awards dinner to be honored with the presentation of the award. Our priest and Johnnie and I attended the affair, held in the magnificent Hotel Patrick Henry ballroom. My wife and I were the only African Americans there. The dinner was delicious, and the formal presentation ceremony was followed by a dance. This was the era of bands, and we had live music. The band played hits of the time, including my favorite, Hoagy Carmichael's silky version of "Stardust": "Though I dream in vain, in my heart it will remain, my stardust melody, the memory of love's refrain . . ."

Johnnie and I danced the night away, not realizing that the Jaycees and their wives expected us to leave after the presentation. I can't remember when we realized this; we just didn't see any other African Americans at the time. A gradual understanding dawned on us after the elegant event was over. The date was December 16, 1965, and we were still living with segregation. Furthermore, we didn't understand that our lives were about to change. At the dance, in another moment of divine intervention, as we paused for a cold drink of punch, one of the Jaycees approached me. He asked if I would be open to joining the organization. I immediately agreed.

I was sworn in as the first African American Jaycee in Roanoke during the first week in January 1966. I was also the first African American to become a member of any White civic group in the city.

Later, I was told that several members had left the organization because a Negro had become a member. It was a big thing at the time. TV cameras came into my seventh-grade classroom to record me at work and document the Black teacher who had joined the Roanoke Jaycees. Thus, I began a fifty-plus-year tenure as a Jaycee. In those years, I met some of the finest young men and women in Virginia and the nation. I visited the homes of White Jaycee members and talked with them and never felt as if my color set me apart. I was a Jaycee working with other Jaycees toward common goals.

The Jaycees had a list of 125 social and civic issues that their members strived to address each year. When I was given the checklist to select a cause for my efforts, there was a blank space by the issue of mental retardation, a term that was later replaced by "intellectual disability." This category appeared to have not been selected for several years. "I'll take it," I said. It was the only one available. It was not an area that I was familiar with, and, at the time, I wasn't sure this would be a good match for me, but I selected it and began to research the field. I wrote the President's Committee on Mental Retardation, established by President John F. Kennedy, to request information and was in contact with local organizations that served this population. It seems as though I was guided to make this choice; it became a major focus of my life's work.

In my first two years as a Jaycee, I involved myself in Christmas shopping tours for disadvantaged children; Punt, Pass, & Kick contests; and other activities. In 1967, I became involved with the Roanoke Area Association for Retarded Children and brought this involvement to the Jaycees. I proposed "adopting" five indigent, intellectually disabled children and using them as our sample group to determine need and how the Jaycees might assist this population.

We took them on shopping tours, to the health clinic, and to sporting events. It was suggested that we gather as many as possible and take them on a picnic. I vetoed that idea with the question, "What happens in the remaining 364 days of the year?" The information we gathered showed that these children and adults needed more physical activity and social outlets. We needed to establish a program of recreation for them.

I knew the director of the Roanoke City Recreation Department. We presented the need for recreation opportunities for this population to the department but were told that there were no funds. I offered to supply the volunteers if the Recreation Department could provide the facility. That was a slam dunk. They agreed to the Eureka Park Center site. There was no shortage of volunteers. Several Jaycees, Johnnie, students from Hollins and Roanoke Colleges, and students from Lucy Addison and Jefferson High Schools signed up to assist, as did local special-education teachers. The press wanted to know how many people were expected for the first Thursday session, and I told them we expected about seventy-five. All of eight showed up. I asked myself what the problem was. Then it hit me. They couldn't get there. I called the bus company. In two weeks, buses were picking up participants at the schools. The number of participants grew to twenty-five, then fifty, and then seventy-five. Dancing, games, and socializing were enjoyed by all. The program needed to expand. A local skating rink provided time on a Saturday for a skating program. The downtown bowling facility allowed us to add a bowling program. The Roanoke Fine Arts Center hosted an arts program. The program grew and grew. At this point, we had programming every Thursday and three Saturdays in the month with more than five hundred people participating.

We requested that the Roanoke City Council provide funds to support the program. The council agreed that the program belonged to the Recreation Department, and the numbers certainly backed up the request. Funds were allocated, and the program was turned over to the Roanoke City Recreation Department.

My next worry concerned what would happen when the schools closed for the summer. I came up with the idea of requesting that the Virginia Jaycees create a summer camp program that would provide to this population what a camp provides to anyone. I also had figured out a way to support it financially. Don Bowles, executive director of the Roanoke Area Association for Retarded

Citizens, pointed me in the right direction. We discussed crafts, an A-frame building, miniature golf, a lake for paddleboating and fishing, basketball and tennis courts, a baseball diamond, and hiking trails. We dreamed big.

In July 1968, I attended the board meeting of the Virginia Jaycees in Virginia Beach. At that time, flanked by Dennis Kuhnemund, national director of the Virginia Jaycees, and Darden Towe, president of the Virginia Jaycees, I proposed to my fellow Jaycees the concept of raising $45,000 to establish a summer residential camp for retarded citizens of the Commonwealth. This concept was put forth after having discussed it with the Virginia Association for Retarded Citizens, as it was then known. The organization had indicated this was one of its top priorities.

I told the Jaycees that I had the perfect manner in which to raise the money. We were going to sell fifteen-cent jars of apple jelly for one dollar. Apples were a homegrown product of Virginia, another plus, I thought. The audience roared with laughter. One Jaycee bellowed that this was the craziest idea he had ever heard of. Another roared that no one in his right mind would make a purchase of this nature at such an inflated price.

I presented the dream to the Virginia Jaycees. We would build a camp for retarded citizens, a way to help provide a better life for these individuals who made up 3 percent of our population, who were Black, White, Jewish, Hispanic, Asian, rich, middle-income, and poor. This condition knew no race, religion, or economic stratum. I knew I had to educate the membership and defend the concept. I knew in my heart the plan would work.

I indicated to all who filled the convention hall that they did not have to worry because once we told individuals that proceeds from the jelly would go toward building a camp for the mentally handicapped, no one would refuse because such a refusal would be tantamount to saying that the person was either against God, country, motherhood, or all three. Even if a person balked at the price, he or she would not want to admit it and would buy the fifteen-cent jar of apple jelly for a dollar. Again, the crowd roared. This time, the roar was in support of me. The group had begun to mellow. I followed by saying that certainly we would be asking for a donation, but we would be giving something in return. I could sense that, even though it sounded crazy, people were beginning to feel that it might work.

Laughingly, one of the Jaycees moved in favor of the proposed project. Another gave it a second, and a third called for the question. The vote by voice was unanimous. However, as the board indicated that evening, the battle had not even begun. There were some 140 chapters in the Commonwealth comprised of approximately seven thousand members. The project would have to be sold at the local level at each chapter. The vote at the convention meant nothing unless this type of follow-through would take place. I agreed that this must and would be done. As the state mental retardation chairman, I would do the selling.

I knew that I needed a gimmick. Returning to Roanoke, I purchased for myself white satin tails, top hat, white gloves, red socks, and a red bow tie. Across the lapels of the suit were written the words: "Apple Jelly Sunday." Thus was born Bill "Apple Jelly Sunday" Robertson. He was the Jaycee missionary who would travel forty thousand miles between September 1968 and March 1969, when the Apple Jelly Sundays would take place. I visited 125 chapters in costume before other organizations and Jaycee groups in North Carolina, Maryland, New York, and Colorado. I wrecked two cars and walked away from them to fulfill speaking engagements. My wife, Johnnie, traveled with me to Jaycee functions, taking her school papers with her to grade at the meetings in order to help keep me awake on the highways or to do the driving herself when I did become sleepy.

Jaycee chapters booked me weeks ahead of time after word of the first two or three speaking engagements got around. Not only was the costume funny and eye-catching, but the speech I had put together was effective. It grabbed at your heart and would not let go. It depicted those who, through no fault of their own, were told to stay in a corner because they were different. I called for Jaycees to extend hands of compassion and care to help bring these individuals out of those corners to be trained, to be loved, to participate in recreational activities, to blend their hearts, minds, intellect, and potential with other Virginians and Americans to make our Commonwealth and nation better places in which to live. I called for Jaycees to make this possible by joining in the drive to bring Camp Virginia Jaycee into being by selling the fifteen-cent jelly. It was a powerful speech, given my Black church background and ministerial style. People stood and applauded to indicate their approval and support. I believed every word I uttered because I was fighting for the underdog. Also, my audiences were mostly White. I was Black, and the people who would most directly benefit were all shades and religions. It was Americans helping Americans. This was my contribution to our great land and our great people.

The appearances were also effective because they attracted the press, newspaper, television, and radio. Soon, Apple Jelly Sunday and Virginia Jaycees were household words.

I remember one Saturday riding in a parade—in my white tuxedo accompanied by retarded children—in Norfolk helping the Jaycees launch their part of the drive. The same afternoon I had to be in Baltimore to speak before the Maryland Jaycees. Between the time I was in the parade and the time I was to catch the United flight out of Norfolk to Baltimore, I did not have time to change clothes. Therefore, I boarded the flight with approximately 125 people aboard. I was dressed in my costume, and a plane full of people were looking at me. I know some of them thought I was crazy. But there were also inquisitive souls who wanted to know what this was all about. I explained that it was a Virginia Jaycees project to establish a residential facility for intellectually disabled children. The Maryland Jaycees had indicated that Maryland state troopers would meet me at the airport. Sure enough, as I stepped from the plane, two hulking Maryland state troopers stepped forward, one taking all the things I had in my hand and the other grabbing me by the arm to weave in and out of the crowd in order to get me to the squad car. While this was taking place, I heard two little old ladies who had been on the same flight. "Gee, he must be a very important person to be met by the Maryland State Police," one said.

"Shush, they are arresting him and taking him away," her companion replied.

On another occasion, I had to be in Culpeper and was accompanied by my son, Allen, who was ten at the time. He went with me on many of these trips. This time it was a Christmas parade, and it was a bit nippy that evening. We were in an open convertible with me dressed in the white tails and top hat. Allen began to cry. "I'm cold," he explained.

"Son, I know you can't be cold because I know your mother put enough clothes on you before we left home," I replied.

"Daddy, I'm cold."

The Jaycee president who was driving the car gave Allen his coat, and not only did my son put the coat over his shoulders but also over his head and sank down into the seat.

I explained all this to Johnnie when we returned home: "Allen might have gotten too cold. We were riding in an open car, and he became cold and the Jaycee president gave him his coat. Allen put it over all of the top portion of his body, including his head, and went to sleep."

Allen replied: "Oh, no, Daddy, none of those things really happened."

"Then, tell us what did happen."

"We were riding in that convertible, and there were lots of people lining the sidewalks and the television cameras were pointed at us. People were taking pictures, and on both sides of our car there were signs reading, 'Buy a jar of jelly to help a retarded child.' Daddy, I was the only child in that car."

I like to tell these stories. They are true. They so vividly point out how we view the condition of mental retardation. Allen didn't want people to think he was retarded. We still have parents who are ashamed to admit they have intellectually disabled children because they feel it reflects on them. We still have too many people who feel the responsibility for disabled individuals rests with parents. These are community problems. We must all share them. We must provide appropriate facilities and services for those who fall into this category.

My children, Allen and Victoria, know what this thing called intellectual disability is all about. They know that education is for everyone. They know that each of us is disabled in some way. They are with me extending their hands and asking those in the corner to come out and join the mainstream.

Getting Jaycee approval and publicizing Apple Jelly Sunday were only the first steps in the project. It was my responsibility to get the jars of jelly to all the chapters in the state. At noon on a Friday in mid-February 1969, I left Roanoke on a forty-foot-long tractor-trailer with a driver, bound for Winchester. There we were to load the jelly, then deliver it to select spots where local Jaycee chapters could pick it up. When we got to Winchester, we learned the truck was not big enough to haul all the jelly. I found a phone to call Roanoke and procure a second tractor-trailer, then began the delivery. My first drop-off point was Charlottesville, scheduled for 10:00 p.m. It had taken the workers so long to load the truck that we didn't get there until 2:00 a.m. There were no cell phones, no way to call the members waiting for me to let them know I would be late. I wondered what I was going to find at the destination. They had waited! Lines of pickup trucks and cars with Jaycees, their wives, and members of the auxiliary group, the "Jaycettes," were there. Such was the case at the next stops at Richmond, in Norfolk, and Virginia Beach. I met the second truck in Lynchburg, delivered there, then to Danville and Bristol, and finally went home to Roanoke. We had saturated the entire state with apple jelly—one hundred thousand jars were delivered!

On Saturday, March 1, the day before Apple Jelly Sunday, the biggest snowstorm in years hit the entire state. What should we do? Phone calls were coming into my home from all over the state. My phone was jumping off the hook. I told them all that the word was "Go." All of our publicity had been geared for that one day. As it turned out, the good Lord blessed us. People were snowbound. They could not go anywhere. Jaycees, Boy Scouts, Girl Scouts, church members, and ladies' group members went from house to house with the jelly. We often heard the remark, "If you're crazy enough to come out on a day like this, I'm crazy enough to buy it."

The Jaycees did not raise $45,000 that day. We raised close to $70,000.

The facility, Camp Virginia Jaycee, officially opened in the summer of 1971 and for the next forty-seven years provided camping experiences for more than forty-seven thousand intellectually and developmentally disabled children and adults.

It should be noted that for the first four years, the director of the camp was a local teacher who only worked during the summer. In 1975, we hired Everett Werness as full-time director. He had a degree in special education from the University of North Dakota. With him in place for more than thirty years, the facility blossomed.

Each generation of Jaycees since then has plugged apple jelly and now apple butter. Camp Virginia Jaycee was realized. A dream came true.

By 1969, I had been selected the Outstanding Young Educator in Roanoke, one of five outstanding young men in Virginia, and the Outstanding State Jaycee Mental Retardation Chairman in the nation. The Virginia Jaycees had honored me with its highest award, the Key Man Award. These accolades had come because of the interest, time, and energy I put into working with youth to prevent school dropouts among the disadvantaged, and providing facilities and services for the mentally handicapped. Because of my work with intellectually and developmentally disabled children and adults, I was recognized with another award: Outstanding Young Man in Roanoke. In 1973, the United States Jaycees named the award going to the chapter in the country with the most outstanding project the William B. Robertson Award.

The camp is one example of mankind in America saying to another segment of mankind in America, "We do care."

9

A FALTERING STEP—
AN INVITING DOOR

My champions during the late 1960s, an era of national change, were Martin Luther King Jr. and Bobby Kennedy. Indeed, Dr. King was the leader on whose shoulders I stood. His work in the area of civil rights was, of course, unparalleled. Attorney General Robert Kennedy, brother of President John Kennedy, was relentless in advocating against segregation and provided support to the civil rights agenda of Dr. King. In 1965, Kennedy was sworn in as a U.S. senator from New York and continued to champion civil rights for all Americans. King and Bobby Kennedy stand at the top of my lists of true patriots.

I was proud to join the list of Virginians on the "Bobby Kennedy for President" Committee headed by former state senator Armistead Boothe of Alexandria. Kennedy announced his candidacy for president in March 1968. I shall never forget his moving address in Indianapolis after the fatal shooting of Dr. King in April 1968 in which he called for racial unity. He spoke from the bed of a truck. In part, he said: "What we need in the United States is not division; what we need in the United States is not hatred; what we need in the United States is not violence or lawlessness; but love and wisdom, and compassion toward one another, and a feeling of justice toward those who still suffer within our country, whether they be white or they be black."

Kennedy's words remain as relevant as they were then. They helped defuse a volatile situation. Indianapolis did not suffer violence that night, but other American cities did. Two months later, in June 1968, Kennedy was assassinated in a hotel kitchen in Los Angeles. I heard the news at 6:00 a.m. as I dressed for school, another shock. I was devastated and could do no more than sit on the bed and cry. Two of my heroes were gone too soon.

My life was in as much of a whirl as the nation. I was very active in the Jaycees program; I was also growing professionally. I became the principal of Hurt Park Elementary School. My school was located in a ghetto area, and I recognized the need to initiate a school breakfast program, which, in time, became citywide. I established the first urban 4-H Club in the city. I had become a very strong advocate of racial harmony, belonging to the city's unofficial biracial committee, the United Fund Board of Directors, and a host of other organizations seeking to promote a climate in which people might live together in unity. I was the first Black citizen in the area to host a weekly television program. It was not geared to a Black audience. *Valley Views* on WRFT television was on at 7:30 p.m. each Monday, prime time, and was oriented to all subjects of interest to the citizens of the Roanoke Valley. Also, I hosted a talk and call-in show, *Your Community Speaks,* on Sunday morning on WTOY geared toward a Black audience. Both programs were extremely popular.

I was much in demand as a speaker on racial matters, politics, intellectual disability, and education. These engagements carried me throughout Virginia and many parts of the country.

Things were going well for me during an exciting period of change. I had become a leader in my own right as Blacks pushed toward the so-called American Dream, and many Whites were looking for someone to tell them what it all meant for Blacks and Whites and for the country.

When integration of schools, public facilities, and other accommodations came to Roanoke, I was asked by city and civic leaders to join with Blacks and Whites to see that it was implemented smoothly. I realized my family and I had been victims of segregation. Even though Black and White children were separated, their worlds overlapped. Our sweet eight-year-old Victoria had seen television advertising about a local amusement park, Lakeside. She saw children her age on the rides seeming to have fun, and she asked to go. There was silence in the room. The commercial changed, and she didn't repeat her request until later, when the commercial came on again. Finally, she was told she couldn't go because of the color of her skin. Fifty years later, she still remembers how shocked she was.

Several White friends asked me why Johnnie hadn't gone to school in Roanoke. They did not even realize that segregation required her to leave home and go all the way to Bluefield to be allowed to attend college. America suffered because of this practice, and I knew my job was to do all that I could to make us see that a divided America was a weak America. I believed strongly that I needed to speak out on Black issues, but always in a manner that would cause people to listen and then do something positive in response to my requests. I was truly a disciple of Martin Luther King Jr. and Gandhi, followers of nonviolence. I became the negotiator, the mediator, the person who felt that America could not and should not be two separate societies. I believed then that things could and would become better for all of us, a belief I still hold. My job was to help bring us together.

Another role I took was as a political activist. In the June 1966 race for the Roanoke City Council, I advised African American voters to single-shot vote. In other words, they should vote for only the Black candidates since the individuals were running as independents. Using the name "Concerned Citizen," I sent a white paper to Black churches and Black civic groups and Black social clubs the weekend before the election explaining this course of action. I was attempting to use every legal tactic possible to give the two African American candidates a level playing field. The Black candidates in that race were Rev. F. E. Alexander, editor of the *Roanoke Tribune,* and A. Bryon Smith, who ran an oil distribution business. They were both outstanding individuals and both registered Democrats, but the Democratic Party would not nominate a Black person, so they had to run as independents. In that election, with few exceptions, White voters would only vote for White candidates. My influence caused quite a stir in Roanoke politics. The Roanoke media played up the issue, asking questions such as, "Why would Robertson advocate such a thing?" "What was Robertson thinking?" I wanted Black candidates winning for a change. At that point, Black lives finally did matter on the local political level.

At a Jaycee meeting in early 1968, the attorney Linwood Holton was the speaker. A prior engagement caused me to be late for the meeting. Upon arrival, I was told that Holton was looking for me. After the meeting, he indicated that he would like to discuss a matter of great importance with me in the near future. I did not hear from Holton for several months. One morning in September of that year, he called and asked if he might come by the school to discuss the matter with me. I told him that would be fine.

Holton indicated that he was going to run for governor of Virginia on the Republican ticket and asked if I would consider running for the Virginia General Assembly on the same slate. This took me by surprise. I was very active in the Democratic Party, and the thought of running for anything as a Republican just did not sit well with me. Holton spelled out the fact that I was "Mr. Virginia," and widely recognized as "outstanding" this and that. I politely explained that I was busy, but I would give the idea some thought. He suggested he would be back in touch.

Johnnie and I discussed this thoroughly. We felt that perhaps this was some sort of publicity stunt the Republicans wanted to pull in order to get a well-known Black in the area to throw support to the Republicans Richard M. Nixon and Spiro T. Agnew, who were running for president and vice president, respectively. I was a member of the Roanoke City Democratic Party and also of the Roanoke City Young Democrats. I was in their ranks and let party leaders know my desire to play a more meaningful political role. I was told there were "plans" for me. I wanted to know where, when, and how, but I received no answers. I felt like I was being overlooked. Was I being overlooked, or was the combination of my race and my perceived arrogance in giving this voting advice blackballing me from involvement in the Democratic Party?

It must be remembered that I was a Bobby Kennedy Democrat and had served on the state committee for his election. Upon his death, the Eugene McCarthy and Hubert Humphrey people began to court me. I told them my head was not in the campaign, and I was going to sit this one out as an active participant.

Holton contacted me again in mid-October, and I told him that I could not give support to the Republican presidential/vice-presidential ticket. He assured me that was not what he was seeking and that I should sit out the election, backing no one. He posed the thought that I was as prepared to run for office as anyone. He wanted me to team with him to bring about a climate in Virginia in which all races, creeds, and colors would feel free and proud to take part. He wanted to know if I felt as strongly about this as he did. One of his main goals was to try to kill the Byrd political machine in Virginia, which had been dominant since the 1890s. Even though Harry F. Byrd Sr., the former Virginia governor and U.S. senator who rigidly stood for White supremacy, fiscal restraint, poll taxes, massive resistance, and regressive taxation, had died in 1966, the Byrd machine was still alive and well, led by Harry Byrd Jr.

I became the first African American in Southwest Virginia to be nominated by a major political party to run for public office. I was on the Republican ticket. African Americans to that point had to run as independents, which gave them little clout. I worked on several of those campaigns. People often ask why I did not run for Roanoke City Council, where I would have been assured a victory. But state law would not permit this because the council had the responsibility to allocate educational funding, including teacher salaries. I was teaching, so if elected, I would have been voting on my own salary. I am not sure I agree with that policy, but it was the law.

Rev. Noel C. Taylor, an African American pastor of High Street Baptist Church, was nominated for the position of city councilman by the Republicans in 1970. He won and served as councilman from 1970 to 1974 and then was named mayor after the death of Mayor Roy Webber. Taylor was the longest-serving mayor in the City of Roanoke, holding that office for more than twenty years. I am hopeful that my candidacy and work played a role in his political career.

In December 1968, I wrote letters of resignation to the Roanoke City Young Democrats and the City Democratic Committee, offering my heavy workload as a reason. I hoped they would write back and request that I not resign but rather cut back on activities for a while or maybe send a letter of thanks. I waited until late March 1969, but nothing came. I called Holton, who had been nominated for governor at a March convention in Roanoke, and said I would be available as a candidate.

My candidacy as a Republican for the Virginia General Assembly was announced in April 1969, with the selection mass meeting to be held in May. The media and the city were asking, "Will conservative Republicans block the nomination of Bill Robertson?"

The night of the mass meeting found the largest turnout ever in attendance. My candidacy had attracted the imagination of the city—Black, White, Republican, and Democrat.

By unanimous vote, I was nominated for one of the two House seats. M. Caldwell Butler, at that time a member of the Virginia House of Delegates from Roanoke, was my running mate. We became fast friends and remained so for many years.

The campaign was on. Johnnie, our children, friends, and neighbors all worked hard for our ticket. "Exciting" and "stimulating" are words that could never begin to describe this period. Speeches, teas, shaking hands, cutting ribbons, and radio and television slots were all part of the whirlwind.

My chances of becoming the first Black man from Roanoke to serve in the Virginia House of Delegates were good, or so said many Black leaders as reported in *Freedom's Journal,* a local Black newspaper.

The night the election returns were tabulated, I was ahead for the first hour or so and then began to fall behind. I lost to a three-term popular Democrat, who was my prime opponent. I always maintain that I ran third in a field of four for two seats. I lost but did not lose. Holton won the governorship. Three days later the newly elected governor called, asking if I would serve as his special assistant for minority and consumer affairs. When you're in midstream, as I was in the currents of political activism, you don't turn back. He did not have to ask twice.

In 1967, Governor Mills Godwin, then a Democrat, came to Roanoke to speak to Roanoke Jaycees at the Hotel Roanoke. I was on the program reporting on the organization's efforts to provide inoculations for measles to prevent disabling conditions among children. He was so impressed that he told members of the Jaycee leadership that he was going to appoint me to an unnamed position.

I went to Richmond in late 1968 to take pictures with Mrs. Katherine Godwin, wife of the Democrat governor of Virginia, who was announcing the shared honorary chairmanship of the Jaycees' Apple Jelly Sunday initiative with Mrs. Muriel Humphrey, wife of Hubert Humphrey. Allen, my ten-year-old son, accompanied me. Dennis Kuhnemund, national director of the Virginia Jaycees, and Darden Towe, president of the Virginia Jaycees, and Mrs. Godwin and I were preparing for the photographers. During this time, Mrs. Godwin mentioned that this would bore Allen and called the office of her husband, the governor, to see if Allen could go over and talk with him. The governor agreed. After the photos, I went to the office and found my son engaged in animated conversation with the governor. He had been a Byrd man and had racist ideas, but he had begun to change and may have wished he had changed earlier. It would be wonderful if I could always remember Governor Godwin as the architect of the state community college system which advanced Virginia educationally and economically and the grandfatherly governor who found time to sit with a little Black child, my ten-year-old son, Allen, and speak with him for an hour and a half. But Godwin was a part of the Byrd institution as a legislator. So many people were hurt, so many children were affected, and sadly, his negative actions are still felt today. We visited briefly. The appointment he had promised earlier was not mentioned. Nothing ever happened. If Godwin had offered me a position or if the Roanoke Democrats had shown concern about me slowing down, would my decision have been the same? We'll never know.

Thus, the offer by Linwood Holton was a godsend. It could not be turned down. In 1967, 1968, and 1969, the Byrd machine was badly crippled, but it was alive. I had never heard a White political leader speak as Linwood Holton had spoken to me. He was offering me a position, if he won, to bring about a new Virginia, a Virginia where equality would prevail. I would play a major role in this. Even though civil rights measures were moving at the national level, state and local change was slow, which made Holton's approach look that much more attractive.

Moderate Republicans such as William B. Poff of Roanoke, Ted Dalton of Radford, and William Wampler of Pennington Gap were people I knew who had fought against school closings. I looked forward to working in closer contact with them. A major issue was that the massive resistance toward integration had closed schools in Newport News, Charlottesville, Norfolk, Warren County, and, for five years, Prince Edward County. The lack of schooling for Black students in Prince Edward County during that five-year period will always remain one of the greatest blemishes on Virginia's history.

The Nixon "Southern Strategy" was to invite the old-school Democrats, like those who supported Byrd, to the Republican Party. These were those who wanted to continue segregation. I was not part of these Republicans. I shared the philosophy of Democrat Bobby Kennedy and Republican Linwood Holton. After forty years of being a Republican, during which time I worked for Barack Obama's campaigns in 2008 and 2012, my state of residence changed in recent years, and I registered as a Democrat. I smiled when I made that change. I no longer wanted to be part of a party led by Donald Trump. Times had changed, and it felt right.

My political party affiliation was secondary to the passion I had for solving the problems of the people in my area. It may have been risky to become a "Linwood Holton Republican," but it was an exciting, fresh opportunity to serve others. It was worth a try.

Hundreds of years from now, when they speak of liberty and equality, they will call the name of Linwood Holton. I am so proud to have been part of his administration.

10

UNPRECEDENTED ENTRANCE TO THE VIRGINIA GOVERNOR'S OFFICE

On January 20, 1970, I became the first Black special assistant to a Virginia governor in the history of the Commonwealth. I knew I could not fail. I made up my mind that I was not going to fail. So much depended on me. If others worked twenty-four hours a day, I would work twenty-five. I knew that being in a position to make a difference was a rare opportunity, and I was NOT going to fail.

The appointment made the news. "Negro Is Named as Aide to Holton," ran the headline in the *Washington Post* on January 14, 1970. A headline in the *Richmond Times* shouted, "Holton Names Roanoke Negro as Aide." The *Roanoke Times* led with, "Robertson First Negro Appointed to Executive Staff of a Virginia Governor."

In his inaugural speech from the state capitol grounds in Richmond in 1970, Gov. Linwood Holton, the first Republican governor in a century, vowed that Virginians would progress through unity. He invoked the name of Abraham Lincoln. I thought I felt the old capitol building shudder; this had never happened before. "Let us now endeavor to make today's Virginia a model in race relations," Holton said. "Let us, as Lincoln said, insist upon an open society 'with malice toward none; charity for all.' Here in Virginia, we must see that no citizen of the Commonwealth is excluded from full participation in both the blessings and the responsibilities of our society because of his race."

Under the grip of the Byrd machine, Virginia still was the leader of the southern states maintaining the status quo with the poll tax remaining in place to keep Blacks and poor Whites from voting, and silencing their voice in state and local governments. Virginia was the leader in fighting the 1954 U.S. Supreme Court decision *Brown v. Board of Education,* and school segregation was the order of the day. While the federal government was chipping away at these dehumanizing laws, segregated water fountains, buses, restaurants, hotels, housing, and other forms of discrimination were used to keep the races apart. Miscegenation laws were in place to prohibit Blacks and Whites from marrying.

Blacks and women were denied equal job opportunities. While some of this had begun to break down, the governors before Holton were disciples of Harry Byrd.

The state was going through a phase known as massive resistance: schools were being closed to keep them from integrating. In Prince Edward County, schools were closed for five years while private and religious schools were opened for White students. Black students lost these years.

This is the atmosphere into which Holton and his people walked. I was the point person to bring about better race relations through job opportunities and equal opportunities under the law. I had never been in government before. Neither had Holton. We were starting from scratch. I felt my background would help me do the job. I knew Virginia geographically and also knew and had interacted with many Black Virginians as well as Whites. My Jaycee contacts proved to be invaluable.

First of all, I had to prove that I was real. There had never been anyone like me in Virginia government. I had to prove myself to people of color. Executive assistant to the governor? What did this mean? How would things change? Was I just someone who would be a yes-man for the establishment and continue pulling the wool over the eyes of the people, or would I really fight to bring about justice and equality for those who had been locked out of the system? With the backing of the governor, I was to see that state agency heads provided opportunities for African Americans and women.

People had to see me, feel me, smell me. Floods of speaking invitations rolled in from churches, chapters of the National Association for the Advancement of Colored People, industry, Virginia's historically Black colleges and universities, and civic groups. Also, White groups wanted to know what all of this meant for them. The governor liked to start his day meeting with his executive assistants. It soon got to the point that I was often absent. I was in some part of the Commonwealth building relationships, selling the governor's program, and seeking assistance for my programming. He and I had to discuss this, and we did. His philosophy was that if something produced results, do it. He felt my work was important enough to allow me to miss some of these meetings.

I questioned how to put my own plan in place. Where would I start? Initially, the governor believed just the weight of the governor's office would open doors. Not so. Most of the department heads were old-line Byrd people who thought Holton would be in office for only one term. Even though Virginia's governors could not serve consecutive terms, they could run for governor in future elections. The remaining Byrd administrators believed they could stall his policies during this term, but I was not going to let that happen. With discipline, patience, and the weight of the governor, I would get things done.

I needed something highly visible to integrate. The public and the agency heads needed to realize that the governor was serious. The Virginia State Police was the department I sought to be my example. There were nearly one thousand state troopers, and not one was Black. The leadership was truly Byrd-influenced. Thus began the saga of Bill Robertson versus the Virginia State Police.

I sat with the commander of the force and got nowhere. That was discouraging. He wanted to maintain the status quo and indicated the force could not find African Americans who were qualified and interested. He felt that if he could hold tight, he would outlast the four-year term of the governor. Others had reported for years that the State Police were running an all-White shop. We needed more effort to recruit Black troopers to make the force a more representative organization.

The governor and I discussed this, and he asked if I could find applicants. My response was "yes," and I went on a twenty-five-consecutive-day recruiting trip, coming home only to get clean shirts and other necessities. I contacted coaches and ministers throughout the state, many graduates of Bluefield State College, and told them what I needed in terms of qualifications for applicants for the Virginia state trooper positions. I asked them to set up meetings statewide, in Southside, Southwest, Central, Tidewater, and the

Eastern Shore to recruit qualified African American males. In no way was I asking that job qualifications be lowered for Negroes. We only recruited qualified applicants and tried to lessen the fear that existed because of past policies. It was a slow process. I returned to Richmond with the completed applications of twenty of the finest young African American men I have ever met. Then they had to take the exam for the State Police force. The first three to take the exam passed it, but the police officials said that they would have to wait because young White men had taken and passed the test before them. At first the excuse was they couldn't find qualified applicants; now it was they would have to wait. I told the officials that the governor would not approve.

When Governor Holton heard this, he called the State Police commander and ordered him to report to the governor's office within the next hour. It was a very short session. The governor told the commander, "Bill told me that three of the men he recruited passed the test."

The commander said, "Yes, Governor, but . . ."

The governor interrupted, called him by name, and spoke emphatically: "No buts. I want them hired tomorrow morning."

By the end of 1971, with three Black state troopers as a starting point, the governor, determined to change this racist mind-set, and I continued working toward our goal of hiring fifteen to twenty Black state troopers. We had started to dismantle the "age of defiance" and to usher in the "aristocracy of ability, regardless of race, color, or creed" described in the governor's inaugural address. Nothing like this had been done before.

New department heads appointed by Holton were more likely to work with me. For example, Rod Layman from Pulaski was appointed head of the Virginia State Alcoholic Beverage Control (ABC) Board by the governor. He was also one of my Jaycee colleagues who knew what the Holton administration wanted. We sat together and worked out a plan to put in place several African American ABC inspectors. The Capitol Police had no Black officers. I worked with the head of the force, and we put in place several Black capitol policemen.

In late 1970, I decided to approach the director of toll-booth attendants in Virginia. This facet of government was also segregated. There were no Black toll-booth workers. I made an appointment to meet with the director at his office on Interstate 95 just outside Richmond.

After introductions, I defined the issue. I pushed by indicating that this would have to change. The director admitted this but indicated that Black people didn't want these jobs. I asked why not. "In the winter it gets so cold and, in the summers, it gets so hot," he said. "Black people do not want these jobs."

I almost fell out of my chair as I listened to this excuse.

For at least an hour and a half, we went around in circles as he stood his ground. "Don't Whites get too hot or too cold?" I asked. Finally, he began to relent and said if I could find someone who met certain qualifications, he would hire him or her.

"Where would I find such a person?" I asked myself. My job was to open doors, but I found more and more that I had to open doors and do the recruiting as well.

I remembered that a recently retired twenty-year U.S. Navy veteran had been in my office a few days before seeking a part-time job. Mr. Dotson's employment for the last three years of his U.S. Navy career was at the Pentagon, where he worked with the chief of naval operations, Adm. Thomas H. Moorer, one of the joint chiefs of staff. "Perfect," I thought. I phoned him and asked him to meet with me. I explained everything to Mr. John E. Dotson Sr.

He was excited and said he was interested. I stressed that the director would attempt to get him to turn the position down with the cold/hot explanation.

He met with the director and called to tell me that he had gotten the position. However, he stated that the director stressed that it was going to be too hot and too cold. Dotson soon became a supervisor, and his success opened the door for other Black employees.

There were other indirect obstacles to hiring Black citizens. The manager of a garment factory was excited about the work we were doing and eager to expand his business by hiring more people. He was hiring mostly Black women and not paying them much but still more than they would make as a domestic, that is, as a maid or housekeeper. Our office worked with him via the Small Business Administration and the local community college, and we were ready to proceed when I got a call from the city "fathers." They wanted to meet me at one of their homes, so I went. There were fifteen White men there who said they couldn't support the shirt factory's expansion. "Why not?" I asked.

They explained that there would be no one left to work in their homes. I was floored, just could not believe it. My job was to fight for minority jobs, to strengthen the economic development of the state, and this was the mentality. But there was progress on other fronts.

Department heads began to hire Black female secretaries. Several were hired for the governor's office. Occupational offices, such as barbering and beauty licensing divisions, began hiring Black inspectors. Times were changing in Virginia. I was excited to be a part of it. I still was delivering twenty-five to thirty speeches per month across the Commonwealth, and it finally felt as if it was paying off. I had something now to report to people, and they wanted to be part of the changes as well. In essence, the message was the same: the Commonwealth and America must embrace the fact that Black lives mattered.

To reach the business community, I developed the concept of Minority Development Career Conferences to be presented across the Commonwealth. The governor sent business leaders invitations to the conferences. Beginning in 1970, we presented ten such conferences, held in Roanoke, Richmond, Bristol, Norton, Charlottesville, Norfolk, Hampton, Martinsville, Northern Virginia, and Accomack. Our team included representatives from the Small Business Administration, Community College System, State Planning and Community Affairs, Education, and State Employment Commission. I, along with the governor whenever he could join these highly successful conferences, stressed our shared goals for Virginia: equal employment and pay for Blacks and women.

Team members from the various agencies would address the business-people in terms of how their departments could assist them in training and recruiting new people relative to their businesses. The conferences would last a day, and of course there would be plenty of time devoted to discussion. Toward the later afternoon, I put forth the question, "How many new people will you hire?" The response was usually positive.

Leonard Creizman, a shirt manufacturer from Ashland who came to the Richmond conference, pledged to hire ten new workers. When he said this, the other business leaders did not want to be left behind, so they began to pledge also. Seeing this, we decided to carry Creizman to all the conferences, and if things got slow, he was to rise and make his pledge. Others followed. The local Virginia state employment office did the follow-up: recruiting and assuring that pledges were honored.

11

HOSTAGE SITUATION

My job responsibilities extended well beyond ridding the state government of job discrimination and changing the attitudes of employers and prospective employees regarding minority employment. I had become a troubleshooter, especially concerning racial issues. At times, I had unexpected opportunities to change attitudes in one-on-one situations.

One memorable occasion took place June 29, 1970. I had been traveling so much that I was behind at work and needed to catch up on correspondence. My desk was piled high with mail from Virginia and from throughout the United States seeking assistance of one kind or another. I had trouble making progress as the interruptions were constant. Between every line spoken into the Dictaphone, the telephone rang or someone came on the intercom with an inquiry or reminder of somewhere I must go or something I must do. The furthest thing from my mind that day was to make a trip to faraway Marion, in Southwest Virginia.

A different sort of call came in at 10:45 that morning. The caller wanted to know if this was William B. Robertson, special assistant to the governor. "Yes," I said, tapping my pen on the desk impatiently. He then informed me that he had a hostage and demanded I come to the Southwestern State Hospital in Marion right away. I knew this was a joke and told

"Tom Drake," as he identified himself, that I was busy and would come tomorrow.

He informed me that this was no joke. He had taken a female nurse. He told me that unless I came to the hospital, he could not guarantee the safety of the nurse. His exact words were: "Do you understand the seriousness of this situation? I have a hostage. Either you come or I cannot guarantee her safety."

I was dumbfounded. "What is this? What can I do? Why me?" The click when he hung up was nearly as ominous as his words.

Via intercom, I told the governor that I needed to see him right away. Slowly I walked the short distance between his office and mine pondering the call. After I explained to him what had happened, he was in a state of disbelief and questioned whether or not I had my facts straight. I assured him that I wished I didn't but was certain I did. To verify the situation, he picked up the phone and placed a call to Dr. Joseph R. Blalock, superintendent of Southwestern State Hospital.

"Blalock, is there a problem there? Is Bill Robertson really needed?" After a lengthy pause, he ended the conversation saying, "He'll be there as soon as he can get there."

Blalock had told him my assistance was desperately needed. A mentally ill inmate had commandeered an office and was holding a hostage. He was a convicted murderer who had killed his father with a tire iron. The inmate was African American, well-built, and highly intelligent. He had adjusted the door lock so it couldn't be unlocked from the outside and barricaded himself in a ground-floor office with a desk and a medicine cabinet pushed against the door. The hostage was a registered nurse, Ola Belle Goldman, who had been dispensing medication.

The governor immediately spoke with Jeanne Ritchie, his appointment secretary, and asked her to arrange to have a state plane readied to fly to Mountain Empire Airport near Marion. He had a dental appointment but said he'd cancel everything else and would be home all evening to help in any way he could. I'll never forget the three emotion-filled words he uttered to me as I left his office to head to the airport: "Please, be careful."

The four-seater Cessna was warmed up and ready to go when I arrived at the airport some fifteen minutes later. The pilot and copilot ushered me aboard, and we took off to the unknown.

The flight took about an hour and a half. A certain amount of anxiety had built up, but I was not afraid. I tried to visualize what awaited me, and then I went to sleep, waking up when I felt the plane touch down. Soon I was stepping out onto the runway, where I was met by two plainclothes investigators for the Virginia State Police. They ushered me to the back seat of an unmarked car and sped to the hospital, briefing me on the way.

I arrived at the hospital at about 1:45 p.m. and met with Blalock and members of his senior staff. Orderlies and nurses and other staff members, visibly shaken and concerned, milled around in the hallway near the superintendent's office. Blalock had announced that no one was leaving the building until this was over, which added to the tension.

There had been a development while I was in flight. A male nurse's aide, Arthur Tilson, had offered to take Goldman's place, and the inmate had agreed. Tilson was the true hero of this story.

Staff members advised me that the inmate exercised regularly and had an IQ of 150 so I should not expect to fool him in any way or to overpower him. He had threatened to kill the hostage if the police or any staff member came near the office. Only I could come, and I must come alone.

The superintendent had not cut off switchboard access for the phone in the office occupied by the inmate. The operator was directed to place all his calls. This was a smart move as it gave us a way to communicate. Before I arrived, the inmate had called several newspapers, including the *Washington Post* and those in Los Angeles, San Francisco, Philadelphia, and New York.

The police wanted to know how I planned to handle the situation. I told them my only choice was to enter the room as directed, alone, and to play it by ear. I emptied my pockets of all contents including my wallet and change and asked Blalock to call the inmate and let him know I was on my way. He did and was warned again that no one else was to come near. I asked everyone to stay clear and began the walk down the corridor to the room where the inmate waited. I was relatively calm, feeling no real fear but rather an uncomfortable sense of uncertainty.

I entered the room about 2:15 p.m. There I found Tilson, a frail, elderly male nurse's aide being held hostage by Ferber James Coleman, nearly six feet tall and weighing about 225 pounds. He looked older than his forty-three years, especially through his eyes. He was a former Marine and looked to be about the size of a football linebacker who had kept in good shape.

Initially, my sole desire was to get Tilson released. I stayed on this issue for a long time. "Let him go home to his family, he has done you no harm," was the theme of my conversation with the inmate until I hit upon the idea of requesting him to release Tilson and make me his hostage.

Coleman was an angry person, angry at the system, hospital, state, life in general. I could see that he would perceive me to be more valuable to him than the current hostage. After much back and forth, he agreed. "I know this is stupid, but I trust you enough to do it," he said. I was able to announce to Blalock that Tilson would be coming out and I would now be the hostage. It was 8:30 p.m.

For the next three or four hours, I did a lot of listening as Coleman vented his anger against everything and everybody. He had filed two appeals regarding his trial, and both had been denied. He was upset about incidents that had happened in the state penitentiary. I was calm and patient and soon saw a weakness in his ranting. If I could secure his transfer from Marion to another facility, would he take it? At this point, he knew that I was the best friend he had. After hours of discussing the trouble he was in followed by an offer of assistance, he accepted my help with conditions—that he not be chained and that he surrender to me and not the Virginia State Police. I explained that the transfer had to be approved by the governor. He agreed that it would be best to leave Southwestern State Hospital. He originally wanted to go to the Virginia Mental Health Institute. There were no maximum-security facilities there, so he agreed to go to Petersburg. Coleman allowed me the freedom to leave the office to confer with the superintendent and phone the governor. Holton gave the OK for him to be transferred from Marion to Central State Hospital in Petersburg without restraints.

The press had been at the facility for some time. I asked that they hold their stories until we could see whether or not there would be a break in terms of the negotiations because my wife did not know where I was and what I was doing. Of course, they had their deadlines to meet. Johnnie, therefore, heard about the situation from the radio and phone calls from friends and relations.

By 11:30 p.m. the State Police placed Coleman in a squad car, and we transported him across the state to the facility in Petersburg, a drive of some five to six hours. I had told the State Police that I did not believe handcuffs were necessary, and Coleman was not restrained. We arrived there around 5:00 a.m. after an uneventful trip. I had been awake for twenty-four hours. However, we had come out of this well. No one had been hurt or killed.

It must be noted that there was never a sense of breaking down the door to apprehend the inmate or a rush after he surrendered to handcuff him or put him in chains. Everyone remained calm, and this kept him calm. It gave talking and negotiations time to work. What could have been a deadly situation ended peacefully. I will always give Dr. Blalock and his staff of mental health professionals credit for creating this atmosphere. Also, both policemen allowed us a peaceful resolution; I sent complimentary letters to their supervisors. I was very pleased with the outcome except for the fact that my wife and children had heard about this via the news media.

12

CELEBRATION

After a year in Holton's administration, I had much to celebrate. The job itself was exciting and challenging. It required me to handle problems ranging from bugs in a jar of tobacco to overcoming racial prejudice. The era was fascinating; a new day was dawning in Virginia. Some would say changes were not coming fast enough, but they were being accomplished in a meaningful way. There was much work to be done, but we had enjoyed successes.

We were making progress in jobs for minorities. Hundreds of commitments for minority jobs had been made for groups, including Spanish-speaking residents of the Washington suburbs and the roughly one million Blacks in Virginia. Jobs ranged from garment workers previously on welfare to supervisory positions in Black-owned businesses. Attitudes were emerging that equated the handicaps women faced in employment to those experienced by ethnic minorities. Training opportunities for all were created and publicized, which added qualified applicants. Regional conferences shared information about programs and resources with employers. Creation of a statewide advisory board helped encourage more open hiring practices. Equally important was changing the mind-set of minority applicants. The old ways were gone, and hiring practices were changing.

Consumer education, another part of my job, was linked closely to minority affairs. The financial issues of the unemployed or underemployed made them easy targets for businesses trying to make a fast buck. We all needed to read the fine print and to know what the interest rates were, especially those with limited finances. I was convinced that more education and greater financial security would lead to economic growth for minorities and for the country as a whole. Although I did not realize it at the time, this philosophy would serve me well in a later role working for the mayor of Washington, D.C.

My family—Johnnie and I and two teenagers—moved to Richmond. Victoria left Lucy Addison to attend Henrico County High School. She declares now that as a high school student with plans that had drastically changed, she was miserable. Allen, a seventh-grader, was a member of the track team, the basketball team, and the choir. Moving also gave him a fresh start escaping from bullies in his elementary school, but he missed school life and friends in Roanoke. Johnnie had opportunities to speak at gatherings, she worked with wives of other appointees, and she taught third grade at Mosby School. We rented our house in Roanoke. Sacrifices were certainly made, but I believed there were more opportunities in Richmond.

Mom remarried during our time in Richmond. She had met her new husband at an AME Church conference. Rev. A. G. Barnes was a pastor in Maryland. As his wife, she became the first lady of his church, a role she handled easily along with her involvement in civic and community events. She walked with me in Richmond, visited my office, and met Holton. Later, she was present when I addressed the Maryland General Assembly. Without a word, her radiant smiles told me how proud she was.

Another positive note during this time was the progress made at Camp Virginia Jaycee. The Jaycees held a ground-breaking ceremony on June 13, 1970, at the site of the 94-acre summer camp for retarded children. Some called it the "Apple Jelly Camp" because of our fund-raising venture. The camp was located between Villamont and Montvale in Virginia and bordered the Jefferson National Forest. The first phase of the camp construction included a central building, a kitchen, a bathhouse with showers, two cabins, playgrounds, and parking facilities. The second phase included a swimming pool and four more cabins. Furniture, equipment, materials, and labor were donated by a variety of businesses. Both phases were completed and ready for the camp season beginning in late June 1971. Roanoke Valley civic clubs funded the fee for many campers at seventy-five dollars each, as did Jaycee chapters all over the state. Several government agencies dealing with children and mental health also provided "camperships," as we came to call the financial support of our campers.

The camp was owned by the Jaycees but administered initially by the Virginia Association for Retarded Citizens and directed by a Bedford teacher, Clarence Mathews. Fifty children from all over Virginia attended the first week and a total of nearly three hundred during the first seven-week camping season. This accomplishment was dear to me, the beginning of the realization of a dream. There were so many memorable campers. Jamie was a thalidomide baby, mentally delayed and without normal arms and legs, but somehow, she could swim. She came to camp every year, unable to speak but full of spirit and joy. Tommie, intellectually delayed, now in his sixties, attended the camp for decades. He was one of the campers who learned the system and worked in the kitchen and earned a check every month during the summer sessions. There was a blind camper who pushed a friend in a wheelchair. "Together," they laughed, "we can find the way." The inspirational stories are endless.

Camp Virginia Jaycee was named the Jaycee Project of the Year in Virginia and one of the top five in the nation. It also received a special commendation from the National Association for Retarded Children and the Joseph P. Kennedy Jr. Foundation. Most important, Camp Virginia Jaycee caught the attention of the White House.

Partly because of my organizational work on Camp Virginia Jaycee, President Richard M. Nixon appointed me to the President's Committee on Mental Retardation (PCMR). The twenty-one-member committee comprised of seven parents, seven volunteers, and seven professionals was charged with assessing the national situation on mental retardation and making recommendations to the president, stimulating and coordinating the work in the field by public and private agencies and all levels of government, and promoting public understanding and action in the field of mental retardation. I was the only Virginian on the committee. Jeannette Rockefeller, Winthrop Rockefeller's wife, was also a member. I was sent across the country, to California, New York, Ohio State University, and the University of Kansas, to establish services and facilities for those with intellectual disabilities. I attended the First Pacific Forum on Mental Retardation in Honolulu as a representative of the President's Committee on Mental Retardation. At that time, I was named

building of our country were not represented appropriately, if at all. Booker T. Washington, who was a young child during the Civil War, was credited with helping to end slavery. African American war heroes like Dorie Miller were not mentioned. In truth, the accomplishments of Black men and women in Virginia were mostly overlooked. Frederick Douglass and Harriet Tubman were ignored. The false claim that thousands of African Americans had served in the Confederate army was taught in these books. The segregation championed for decades in Virginia was not mentioned. Seemingly pro-Confederate by design, these works were written by the authors of children's books, not historians.

The public pressed to get rid of these texts, and, in 1972, the governor's staff got involved. I told the Virginia Board of Education that these were "excellent examples of propaganda." I explained that I did not want to refight the Civil War, "but these books needed to be gone immediately."

Previously, I had criticized the texts at a human resources seminar of the U.S. Jaycees in Flint, Michigan, and asked that Virginia's textbooks all be scrutinized in such sensitive areas as the history of slavery and accomplishments of heroic Black Americans. "History books have done a grave disservice to Black Americans and all schoolchildren by not mentioning people like Dorie Miller. Black, White, and Red men have always been fighting and exploring together for what we all love and want to possess—freedom." The governor allowed them to be phased out over a period of a few years. It was a triumph, albeit a long, drawn-out one.

Another priority was to present to the public a message that would inspire change in the field of social and racial inequities. I spoke more than one hundred times per year to groups as varied as the National Association for the Advancement of Colored People (NAACP), the American Association of University Women (AAUW), the King and Kennedy Day Care Center, colleges, and to both Black and White civic groups.

My efforts were recognized in my hometown in March 1971 as Roanoke mayor Rob Webber proclaimed "Bill Robertson Day." The theme for the day was "How Precious the Gift of Self." A number of well-known people came to participate in the testimonial banquet that climaxed the day at the Hotel Roanoke. Hundreds of dinner guests attended.

Robert J. Brown, special assistant to Nixon, and Berkley G. Burrell, president of the National Business League, joined the keynote speaker, an editor of

Reader's Digest, James Daniel. More than a dozen other leaders of businesses, churches, and civic groups, including the Jaycees, took the stage to express their appreciation. The master of ceremonies remarked that it took a table sixty feet long to include those making tributes. Holton wrote: "You have been a builder of bridges, enabling people of various backgrounds to understand each other by helping qualified minorities gain jobs where opportunities did not exist before."

I was humbled by the attention and thrilled that donations and proceeds from the event were presented to the Virginia Association for Retarded Children and Camp Virginia Jaycee. An especially poignant advertisement in the event program read "In Honor and Appreciation of 'OUR' BILL ROBERTSON—Tidewater Association for Retarded Children."

I was overwhelmed.

13

HOT SUMMER IN HILL CITY

All was not celebration. There was tragedy and sadness. Stanley, my next-youngest brother, with whom I had shared much of my life, was shot and killed in 1972 at thirty-seven years old. I often thought that if Daddy had still been alive, Stanley's death would have killed him. Stanley was much loved by all, but especially by our father. He was six foot six, a star basketball player at Lucy Addison High, and a former Marine. Most of all he was full of fun, a jokester. I felt like a part of my life was lost with his death, but life went on.

A speaking engagement in May 1972 carried me to Roanoke, where a message awaited me at the Holiday Inn: two Black leaders from Lynchburg wished to see me after the speech that evening.

The meeting took place in a private residence. I was locked inside, and the men suggested that I would not be able to leave until there were solutions. They meant business. The two individuals painted a picture of a "hot summer" in the Hill City of Lynchburg, where dissatisfaction over the lack of jobs for Black youths ages fourteen to twenty could erupt into violence. A summer jobs program was needed in order to channel the energies of these youths into something positive.

To verify this, I checked with the Virginia Department of Human Resources, which monitored such situations in the Commonwealth. The response was, according to information they had compiled, that the Hill City was one of five places in which trouble could be expected that summer.

The department and I began to identify sources from which money could be found to create a program to serve disadvantaged young people. The search took place in Washington and Richmond. We did not want to provide false hope in Lynchburg until we were certain money would be available.

However, while we were in the process of locating funds, I received a call from the mayor of Lynchburg, who was attending a conference in New Orleans. Someone had casually remarked to him that hopefully his problems in Lynchburg could be resolved and that money would be forthcoming. "What problem?" was his immediate response. He was infuriated when he spoke to me, indicating that Lynchburg did not have any problems and that he had to travel all the way to New Orleans to hear something about his city that was not true.

Though he was wrong in saying or believing there were no problems, I could understand how he must have felt. He indicated very strongly that he and his city did not need assistance nor would it be accepted.

During June of that year, I made three trips to Lynchburg to confer with the mayor; the mayor and White leaders; the mayor and Black leaders; and the mayor and Black and White leaders. Funding had been found to put the employment program into effect. However, the mayor had to write a letter to Holton requesting the money, which would amount to approximately $50,000, to put more than 150 youths to work.

The mayor was still angry, and he and I discussed the merits of the program for over an hour. There would be no program unless he requested the money in writing. "Let's go in to my secretary, you dictate the letter to her, and I'll sign it," he finally said to me. The program was born. Possible unrest was averted. Lines of communication were opened between the Black and White communities. The mayor and I developed a rapport and genuine respect for one other.

14

VIRGINIA STATE PENITENTIARY

My appointment book page for December 12, 1972, was full. It was to have been a routine day for me dealing with consumer complaints and helping people seeking jobs. In no way was I prepared for what was to take place later in the day.

A secretary passed the office and asked if I had heard of the disturbance at the state penitentiary. I had not and had no time to even inquire about the matter. I continued with my daily schedule until just before noon, when a call came from Otis Brown, secretary of Welfare and Institutions, who asked if I would take a ride with him to the Virginia State Penitentiary.

He explained that there had been a disturbance in the prison mess hall that morning after inmates had been informed that a fellow prisoner had been beaten by several guards the night before. Addison Slayton, the penitentiary superintendent at that time, had talked with the inmates along with Chaplain Walter Thomas. The men had been persuaded to move to the chapel. As I understood it, initially there were 100 to 150 men involved. By the time I was informed, that number had grown to 400. The inmates were asking to speak with the governor, and when told that was impossible, they asked to talk with me.

I almost knew what to expect because along with Thomas, who was stationed there, and the Rev. George Picketts, who was in charge of the chaplain's service, I had been telling prison officials they were sitting on a powder keg and the lid was going to blow off if they did not act in a positive manner. A pipe bomb had been made in the prison and had exploded. Complaints about brutality were frequent. We had discussed the general mistreatment of inmates and made recommendations for improved conditions. We wanted prisoners to return to society as productive citizens. All this had fallen on deaf ears.

I told Brown that I would not try to deal with 400 men but rather would meet with a committee representing the inmates. Therefore, the inmates formed an ad hoc committee to meet with prison officials and me. The committee was comprised of five Black inmates and five who were White, men whom I came to admire as we worked together. After selecting their committee and before I arrived, the inmates hastily jotted down their list of grievances.

Arriving at 500 Spring Street at the antiquated prison in early afternoon, I found in the conference room the ten-man inmate committee, the prison superintendent, the chaplain, and others on the staff. Several of the inmates I knew because of earlier visits I had made to the institution with the governor. After shaking hands all the way around, the inmates presented a list of some thirty-five to forty-five grievances. This list would grow to seventy-three before my stay was ended. The grievances covered a wide range of concerns:

- Improved recreational opportunities
- More showers with access that did not require going outside
- Showers on every tier
- More inmates on work-release programs
- Conjugal visits
- Fewer early lock-ups
- Opportunities to listen to radios
- More and more varied reading materials in the library
- Lights in cells
- More opportunities for haircuts
- Psychological tests for personnel
- Inmates being assigned a facility close to home to allow family visits
- Hot water in the mornings
- Improved medical care

- Right to legal counsel at parole hearings
- Opportunities to watch television
- More Black officials

In my estimation, many of these items were due to any human being. One additional grievance that was not debatable was the removal of Captains Rufus Baker and G. E. Mitchell, who were constantly referred to as "brutal."

After approximately two and a half hours of negotiation, I asked the inmates to give prison officials and me several days to consider the grievances. I was attempting to buy time as the committee pressed for a deadline. I pulled a figure—ten days—out of the air.

The committee was agreeable, but they could not speak for the 400 men in the chapel and asked if I would present the plan to the other men and seek approval of the larger group. I was reminded that it would be difficult to get anything done if Baker and Mitchell were not removed. One inmate said they could not guarantee the guards' safety if they remained. I then instructed prison officials that for the sake of successful negotiations the two men must be removed from the yard at least for the ten-day period. It was then I learned that Hunter Jackson, an assistant superintendent, was still in the chapel. I was not certain whether he was a hostage. News reports later said he was. Sources close to the scene indicated he was not. I told the inmates when I came out that Jackson was to come out as well. They agreed. Slayton, Thomas, and I entered the chapel, where Slayton spoke to the men, indicating that the special assistant to the governor was there and would speak to them. The men roared their approval. It was clear they believed Slayton had acted in good faith.

I outlined what had been discussed. A representative of the inmate committee asked if I would continue to work with prison officials and the inmate committee while attempting to build up goodwill for their plight on the outside. I agreed, and the men gave this plan of action an overwhelming endorsement. The press was at the doors, and the prison officials and I determined that Slayton and I would speak to them.

Slayton briefed the press on what had transpired, and I indicated that some changes could be made. Also, I indicated to the members of the press that on Friday, December 22, 1972, a group comprised of prison administrators, inmates, and me would hold a press conference to explain how each grievance was handled. Reporters had received copies of the grievances. During these hours, one hundred state troopers had been stationed at the nearby War Memorial Building. Thankfully, they were not needed.

In reporting to Holton, I told him that many of the grievances could be taken care of with little or no money but rather with imagination, innovation, and good faith on the part of prison officials. "There are a million and one reasons that could be given why something could not be done, but very few could be offered as to why things should be done," I told him. Holton called Secretary Brown at the Department of Welfare and Institutions, who had summoned me initially, and said that he wanted positive action and not excuses.

This began ten days of the most delicate negotiations in which I have ever been involved. The prisoners saw hope in me because I was from the governor's office and a Black person who operated from a base of power and could feel some sensitivity for them. On the other side they saw prison officials who were concerned but did not relish the idea of the governor's office being involved so closely. In addition, prison staff wanted to assume that since the initial crisis was over, they could go back to business as usual. I informed them that business as usual was over. A commitment had been made, and it would be honored.

The credibility of the governor's office was on the line, and I was being tested to see if a high-ranking Black state official would be allowed to function the way a White official would have been. I explained that my word was valuable and they would not be allowed to take it lightly.

For the next two days, I met with prison officials and the committee. Progress was being made, but it came to a halt on December 14, when a press release went out from the administrators of the prison indicating that guards had not unduly attacked any prisoner, giving the impression that the administration was without fault. It was quite clear that prison officials were disregarding one of the ground rules set up during the initial stages of negotiation. It had been decided that neither the inmates nor the administration would issue press releases. We recognized that issuing releases, especially those containing half-truths, would aggravate a very sensitive situation. Also, prison officials could easily get to the press, but inmates could not, so inmates yelled from the windows to the reporters waiting outside. I asked that no additional information be sent to the press from either side.

During this time, with committee members working feverishly with both the prison and higher-level administrators to put into precise language the responses to the grievances, it was brought to my attention that while we were meeting that first day, damage had been done to the commissary, and locks had been broken in Cell Block A. Because of the broken locks, men were moving from A cell house to B cell house. Official counts were impossible. Only a small percentage of the inmate population was involved, but the situation represented danger to the population as a whole.

On December 18, prison officials, the secretary of the Commonwealth, assistant attorney general, and I met in the conference room of the director of Welfare and Institutions in order to figure out how the problem of the locks would be solved. The meeting convened just after lunch and did not adjourn until close to midnight. It was proposed that state troopers be brought in to man the cell blocks until the locks were secured. Locksmiths wanted protection inside the prison. Rumors were flying that some inmates were not going to allow the locks to be fixed. I was one of several who did not want to see the State Police brought in, but I finally gave in after no positive alternative could be found. I felt we were again breaking faith with the inmates. Because of the actions of a few, we were going to bring in 200 state troopers under the cover of darkness. This also would put the members of the committee in a bad situation, making it appear as if they were serving as liaisons between the inmate population and the administration.

I asked that I be allowed to enter the cell blocks early in the morning of December 19 after the troopers were in position to inform the prison population that nothing was to be feared and the troopers were only there to see that the locks were replaced. We had been told it would take about eight hours to complete the job. However, all the parts could not be easily found, and it took some thirty hours.

Many of the inmates were upset because of the presence of the state troopers; others felt relieved. Many indicated they were happy that I had entered the cell blocks to provide information. This meant a great deal to me because my credibility was at stake again. It took the committee members off the spot and gave us the element of trust to continue our delicate talks.

All did not go smoothly with negotiations. Several times the prison administration said it did not have time to meet or had little time. I pushed for as much time as possible and met with the administration every day. The inmate committee could not agree on some of the suggested solutions. My role was to pull everyone, inmates and administrators, together. There were separate meetings for inmates to come up with their solutions and administrators to come up with theirs. The joint meetings were conducted to put items together or throw them out, rehash them, or start over. There were frustrations, light moments, and bitter exchanges. But the mandate was clear: by Friday, December 22, we must come up with a final draft that all could live with and build upon to open new lines of communication and start true rehabilitation within the penitentiary.

It was evident at this time that some decisions would not please all the inmates. At the same time, many people on the staff were beginning to feel threatened because seemingly a great deal of attention was being paid the prisoners. This was interpreted correctly to mean that the old and entrenched ways of doing things were changing, that the status quo no longer would be maintained. One of the big failures of the administrators was that they did not work with staff to reassure them and to make all feel that it was time for changes and that all could work toward these changes together.

Instead, there was a steady buildup of staff-inmate resentment. This was natural, but prison officials could have handled it in a more positive manner. My responsibilities were too great at the time in seeking to keep the lid from blowing off to concern myself with the staff's self-esteem. Evidently, I was a symbol of all that was taking place and would have to deal with staff also.

On the morning of Friday, December 22, the tenth day, a thirteen-page document was finalized that answered the inmates' grievances. It stated that inmates would be treated as human beings with the rights to showers, television, lights, radios, and minority input at the administrative level. Medical experiments using inmates would cease, a permanent inmate committee would meet with prison officials, the press would be allowed to interview inmates, there would be access to improved recreation opportunities, and additional vocational and educational courses would be made available. It did NOT state that prisoners would control the facility.

That day, William Lukhard, director of Welfare and Institutions; Slayton and Thomas; the ten-man inmate committee; and I sat down with the media from Virginia and other parts of the nation to discuss our progress. This was done openly and candidly and was termed "unprecedented" by the media. This was the Christmas present I wanted for all concerned. The Attica prison uprising in New York had claimed forty-three lives a year earlier, yet none had been killed in our situation in Virginia. We had acted in a responsible manner. We had come up with short-term and long-term goals. We were on the way to rehabilitation, but I knew this was not the final episode.

The plans for television viewing and some other issues were put into effect right away. It was then I discovered that prison officials were not living up to commitments to put into operation other items we had decided upon. They did not want to recognize an inmate committee. They procrastinated on many of the items. I was called back in January 1973 to reopen lines of communication. The staff closed their eyes to many things that were taking place.

I had learned that you cannot work with inmates unless you work with staff. I had gotten that opportunity on December 26. Guards at the penitentiary asked me to meet with them. I was presented with a list of their demands, which included higher salaries and their opposition to a committee of inmates being allowed to recommend dismissal of any guard. Captains Mitchell and Baker were not dismissed but reassigned. Mitchell was reassigned temporarily and then returned to the prison yard. The staff grievances were presented to prison officials and the governor just as those coming from the inmates had been.

Prison officials did not lose control of the penitentiary. They did fail to fulfill some of their responsibilities by turning the other way or tuning out what they did not want to hear.

At the time, there were personnel in the state penitentiary and the penal system throughout the Commonwealth who not only would have liked to see a full-scale prison riot but would have encouraged it in order to return to what will never be in existence again: the old system. They wanted to rule completely and give the inmate no voice. There are those who say the only way to treat those people is to use brute force. There are those who say not to negotiate with inmates.

"We need someone who will kick butt, go home and eat ice cream and not worry about it, and go back and kick butt again tomorrow," I told Holton. I wanted to bring in a new assistant superintendent, and I had someone in mind, Joe Lewis, a Bluefield State College graduate. At that time, there were no Black officials at the prison. He was coaching at Kittrell College in North Carolina, but we managed to lure him away. He helped improve conditions at the Virginia State Penitentiary and the overall operation of Virginia's penal system. We shared ideas about the changes that were needed. Joe once remarked to me that my work and that of the governor "had changed the color and character of the government of the Commonwealth of Virginia." Joe Lewis became the first ranking African American in the state's penal system.

The vast majority of those confined go back into society, but while they are in the care of the state, they must be given every vocational and academic opportunity possible. They must come back to our communities not more hardened but eager to work within the framework of society. This will never take place if the attitudes of those who represent prison administration and staff do not reflect belief in human dignity.

William Bernard Robertson (*right, standing*) with fellow graduates at Lucy Addison High School, Roanoke, Virginia, 1950. (William B. Robertson Papers, Archives Collection, Bluefield State College)

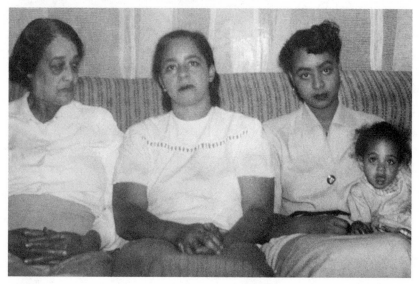

Robertson's maternal grandmother, Mary Roberts; mother, Rebecca Robertson; sister, Faye Robertson; and her daughter, Wadine Toliaferro, 1949. (William B. Robertson personal collection)

Ruth Price and William (then known as Bernard) Robertson, Senior Prom, Lucy Addison High School, Roanoke, Virginia, 1950. (William B. Robertson personal collection)

Kickoff event for the Virginia Jaycees' Apple Jelly Sunday at the Virginia governor's mansion, 1968. *Left to right:* Mrs. Katherine Godwin, First Lady of Virginia and honorary cochair of the program; William B. Robertson; Darden Towe, president of the Virginia Jaycees, 1968–69; and Dennis Kuhnemund, national director of the Virginia Jaycees, 1968–69. (William B. Robertson Papers, Archives Collection, Bluefield State College)

Virginia Governor Linwood B. Holton signs a proclamation establishing a State Office for Minority Business Enterprise to be located at Virginia State College, 1972. Witnessing the signing are (*from left*) B. F. Dabney, director of the VSC Office of College Relations; John L. Jenkins, national director of the Office of Minority Business Enterprise, Department of Commerce; William B. Robertson, special assistant to the governor for minority affairs; and Dr. Huey J. Battle, chairman of the VSC Department of Economics and director of the Bureau of Economic Research and Development at VSC. (VSC photo by D. C. Youkeles. William B. Robertson Papers, Archives Collection, Bluefield State College)

Governor Linwood Holton with officials from the National Business League (which predates the U.S. Chamber of Commerce). *From left:* William B. Robertson, special assistant to the governor of Virginia; Berkeley Burrell, president, National Business League; Governor Holton; and Val Washington, grandson of Booker T. Washington. (William B. Robertson Papers, Archives Collection, Bluefield State College)

William B. Robertson, special assistant to the governor of Virginia, on the steps of the Virginia State Capitol Building in Richmond, 1971. (William B. Robertson Papers, Archives Collection, Bluefield State College)

Everett Werness, director of Camp Virginia Jaycee, 1975–2017, with a camper at a Roanoke Kiwanis fund-raiser at and for the camp, August 2006. (Photo provided by Everett Werness)

President Richard Nixon and members of the President's Committee on Mental Retardation, 1972. Robertson is second from the right. (William B. Robertson Papers, Archives Collection, Bluefield State College)

Barbara Bush on a visit to Camp Virginia Jaycee, 1988. She met teachers from South Africa, Kenya, and Sierra Leone who came to share their ways of teaching and to develop curricula from American models. (William B. Robertson Papers, Archives Collection, Bluefield State College)

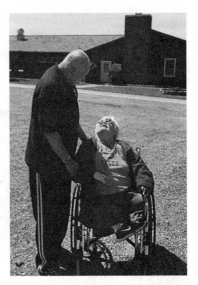

Ruth and William B. Robertson at their home in Tampa, Florida, May 2006. (William B. Robertson Papers, Archives Collection, Bluefield State College)

Camp Virginia Jaycee founder William B. Robertson with Jamie, a camper who had been a thalidomide baby, intellectually delayed and without normally developed arms and legs, 2017. She came to camp every year for decades, unable to speak but obviously happy to be there. (Photo provided by Victoria Robertson)

The president of Bluefield State College, Dr. Marsha V. Krotseng; William B. Robertson; and Victoria Robertson seated in front of a group of young men from Sligh Middle School in Tampa, Florida, 2015. These "Men of Vision," sponsored by Robertson, were visiting Camp Virginia Jaycee and Bluefield State College in West Virginia. (Photo provided by Victoria Robertson)

The first of a million books to be distributed in Africa by CHEER (Center for Health, Education, and Economic Research) are delivered to Hanover Primary School in Bhisho, Eastern Cape, South Africa, 1994. Shown here are the provincial minister of education (*left*), and William B. Robertson, (*right*), along with students, teachers, parents, and pensioners. (William B. Robertson Papers, Archives Collection, Bluefield State College)

Bernice Victoria Robertson, 2020. (Photo provided by Victoria Robertson)

Allen and Cynthia Robertson, 2004. (William B. Robertson personal collection)

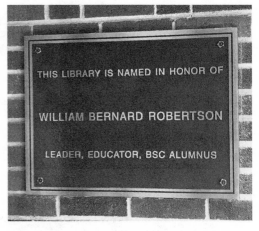

This honorary plaque at Bluefield State College Library was unveiled at the ceremony to rename the school's library after Robertson, August 2019. (William B. Robertson personal collection)

Eva and Teddy Robertson, 2013. (William B. Robertson personal collection)

Dr. Garry Moore, chairman of the Bluefield State College Board of Governors; William B. Robertson; and Dr. Robin Capehart, president of Bluefield State College, following the ceremony to rename the college library after Robertson, August 2019. (Photo provided by James Leedy)

15

HAVES VS. HAVE-NOTS

On May 30, 1973, the thirteen-year-old son of the governor of Virginia was the victim of an attempted robbery. I found out the next day when Governor Holton asked if I would step into his office. He told me about Woody being accosted by several Black youths who had demanded money from him while he was delivering his afternoon newspapers. Woody, who is White, convinced them that he had no money, which was true, and they cuffed him some more and let him go. Woody was not hurt. He was more frightened than anything else.

The governor explained that things were out of his hands. Once a member of the governor's family is set upon or the governor is attacked, it becomes a matter for the Virginia State Police. He requested that I lend support in whatever manner I could. That afternoon, as Woody delivered his papers followed by two Virginia State Police troopers in plain clothes, I also followed.

Near the end of his route and on the fringe of a Black neighborhood, two young boys about Woody's age, who were among the attackers of the day before, approached him, demanded money, and pushed him around. The state troopers moved in after Woody gave the boys three marked one-dollar bills. They were apprehended with the goods on them and the policemen as witnesses and were arrested. I also was a witness, standing on the corner not too far away, pretending to be reading a newspaper. Neither Woody, the police, nor the young culprits knew I was there.

I was able to get the boys' addresses and recognized that the youngsters had come from the adjoining neighborhood. I visited the area. What I found was poverty in its worst form. Drab, dreary homes each housing two or three families, dusty backyards leading to an alley, young girls sitting on stoops with babies in their arms. None of the niceties of life were visible. I thought to myself, how many times have I seen this sight? As a former schoolteacher in a ghetto area, and even in my own neighborhood, I was all too familiar with this scene. Crime is never the answer to this type of situation. Yet, this atmosphere breeds crime.

The next day I reported to the governor and told him I wanted to give thought to some type of activity that would counter this negative action. He gave me the green light. The next day, the governor, his wife, two daughters, Woody, and an entourage of aides, including me, left Richmond for Lake Tahoe, Nevada, for the states' governors conference. We were to stay four days.

Woody and I had time to talk during a long plane ride and a long car ride. We thought in terms of what we could do to turn a bad situation into one that could be positive. We both knew that if two young Black men were moved to robbery because they could not find employment or had not been taught the value of work, surely there must be many others in the Richmond area with the same problem.

First, I wanted Woody to see the living environment of the youngsters himself when we returned. We talked of getting in touch with the business community and city officials to see if help could be gained. When we returned, Woody and I made a visit to the area and saw the dilapidated houses. The two youths, along with others, were playing basketball in a dust bowl in the continuous backyard. They were leery of this White newspaper boy who had gotten them in trouble and this big, hulking Black male. They truly did not know who Woody was, and they assumed that I was a policeman. They did not know who the governor was, nor did they realize the seriousness of their actions. It was something that came naturally. Woody had, and they didn't. That was the extent of it.

We gained their confidence when the basketball came my way and I sank a jump shot from ten feet out. Woody, who showed no fear at all, picked up the ball for a layup. Our basketball play brought high fives and slaps on the back. The next day, we went back and played with the group. We had been accepted.

Woody thought about the situation and told an interviewer at the governor's mansion, "Hey, I have all these privileges and they have practically nothing, nothing but to roam the streets and get into trouble."

Next, I wanted the boys to see where and how Woody lived. The two youths who robbed Woody were awaiting trial. The robbery charge was based on the second confrontation as nothing was taken in the first incident. One was twelve and the other was fourteen. We talked with them about the state capitol and the governor's office. Even though the capitol was only about twelve blocks from their neighborhood, it could just as easily have been a million miles away. We asked the boys and their friends if they would like to visit, and a big shout of "Yes!" went up.

We told them to be ready the next day at 2:00 p.m. We had the Capitol Police line up five cars to pick the children up and take them back; Woody and I rode with them both ways.

When we arrived, there were approximately twenty-five children waiting for us, ranging in age from six months to fifteen years old. We loaded them in the cars and drove to the capitol. We walked them around the capitol building with all of its marble and ornate architecture. Glaring from the walls at them were portraits of old-line segregationist governors who would not have approved of their presence there. Perhaps for the first time, those who had robbed Woody and others were riding in police cars but not going to jail. They were going to the office of the governor himself.

The children were ushered into the governor's conference room, where they sat in the comfortable cushioned chairs. The plushness was noticed with "oohs" and "ahhs." I sat the six-month-old baby in the chair that read "Governor of the Commonwealth of Virginia." It represented change; that infant represented not only the future of Blacks in Virginia but the future of Virginia and America. This Black child could become a future governor.

The next step was to have Woody meet with the business community to relate what he had learned and seek assistance. Letters signed by Woody were sent to business leaders inviting them to a meeting at the John Marshall Hotel. The session was well attended, and Woody told all what had happened. He added that there were more inner-city children in the same situation as these. He stated that working together in a public/private partnership we could change some of these situations. His idea was to provide jobs for as many of these young people as possible. Woody ended his speech before the group of businessmen by saying, "You can pay a little now or a whole lot later." This reference was to the state penitentiary located a few blocks away from the hotel.

The business community contributed forty-five thousand dollars to what became known as "Woody's Job Corps." The mayor of Richmond was at the meeting and pledged support in the form of expertise, trucks for pickups, garbage cans, shovels, and brooms. The Richmond Urban League, Richmond Community Action Program, National Association for the Advancement of Colored People, churches, and others became part of the effort and provided supervision and lunches. They enabled us to put 103 disadvantaged Black and White youngsters to work cleaning up their neighborhoods for the summer. They were paid twenty-five dollars each week with a few dollars held back each week to buy school supplies and clothes in September.

It was a highly successful program. Absenteeism was almost nonexistent. The youngsters worked with zeal and pride. Woody went out to work with them. The alleys and vacant lots and streets were cleaner.

"Keep Virginia Beautiful" reported the program to "Keep America Beautiful." As a result, Woody and the two young men who attacked him and another ten members of the corps were invited to New York, where "Keep America Beautiful" was hosting an awards program. The emcee, Shirley Temple Black, presented an award to the Richmond group. Accepting the award were Woody and the two young men. Because of their involvement in the work program, the two youths were paroled to their parents.

Who says problems cannot be resolved? Children stuck in poverty cannot be wished away. They are the responsibility of us all. Remember, we can pay a little today or a whole lot more tomorrow.

Solving any problem can be more efficient and effective when all those involved are brought together and are comfortable sharing ideas and visions. Integration means bringing the best one has to mix with the best someone else has to create a situation in which the combination will bring about a new start for both parties.

This is what had been envisioned for the schools of Virginia and America when the *Brown v. Board of Education* decision was rendered. However, this was not the case in school districts throughout the United States. Old hatreds, or, perhaps better stated, old fears, began to surface.

During my tenure in the office of the governor, I was constantly called by people of goodwill, both Black and White, to enter their communities where unrest was taking place to negotiate compromise that would lead to better understanding. This was always done without the benefit of press and other fanfare.

In each of these situations, I would enter a community upon the request of concerned citizens, meet privately with the superintendent of a locality, the mayor, and then with the concerned group. Next, I would meet with Black parents, then White parents, then conduct a joint meeting with both. The next step was to meet with student leaders, Black and White, always listening, then suggesting ways in which people could work together in order to better understand each other.

Finally, I would meet with members of the business community to impress upon them that racial unrest left unchecked could ultimately disrupt a community educationally, socially, and economically. Upon leaving these areas, I would help to set up biracial committees to deal with problems. All facets of the community were now involved.

Generally, it would take five consecutive days to bring about the type of climate I sought to initiate. It was always worth the effort. At least five areas in Virginia and several in other states were assisted in this manner.

There is still much to be done in this area in our country. While I do not suggest there are simple solutions to our problems, I do say that in most instances we are saying the same things. However, each side is shouting so loudly that it cannot hear the other. Someone who really cares must be there to make certain that the shouting is dialed down enough for people to hear and begin to set common goals and objectives. That can mean the difference between a community that is divided and one that is attempting to come to grips with its problems.

16

A VOICE FROM
THE NAACP

Linwood Holton was the first southern governor to work with the National Association for the Advancement of Colored People (NAACP) to bring about equality for all Virginians. Our administration interacted with people of high integrity such as Oliver Hill, Sam Tucker, Henry Marsh, and Lester Banks, leaders of the state organization in Richmond, as well as the national headquarters in New York at that time.

In my last year in the governor's office, the Virginia NAACP convention was to be held in Fredericksburg. Banks, the Virginia NAACP director, called to see if I would assist in getting Holton to honor the national director, Roy Wilkins. I assured him of my willingness to help. He went on to say that the Virginia NAACP wanted to honor the governor for his almost four years of leadership. I made the necessary arrangements.

Wilkins was revered by civil rights advocates. He was a leader in the NAACP as executive secretary from 1955 to 1963 and executive director from 1964 to 1977. Days prior to the convention, local NAACP officials brought him by my office, where he paid me the ultimate compliment.

I told him that right after my graduation from Bluefield State College and the horrific lynching of fourteen-year-old Emmett Till in 1955, I had written to the NAACP requesting a field position but never heard from the organization. Emmett was from Chicago and was visiting family in Mississippi. He was accused of flirting with a White woman. Witnesses say that he said, "Bye, bye, Baby," to her. The woman's husband and his half brother kidnapped young Emmett from his great-uncle's house in the wee hours of August 28, 1955. They beat him severely and shot him in the head. They threw his body in the Tallahatchie River. Despite their efforts to weigh the body down with a large cotton gin fan, it surfaced three days later, so bloated and disfigured that the boy had to be identified by a ring on his finger.

The men were found not guilty because the jury believed that the state failed to prove that the disfigured body was Emmett. Many years later, the woman who accused him recanted her story. The outrage following Emmett Till's murder and trial partly fueled the passion that sparked the civil rights movement. I had been ready, at that time, to devote my life to supporting civil rights. Instead, I taught school, I started a camp for the disabled, I worked in the governor's office, and it was two decades later.

Roy Wilkins never missed a beat. "Of course, you did not hear back," he answered. "The national organization knew that Linwood Holton would come along in 1970 and select you as the special assistant who would make such a difference in the lives of those left out of the system, and the organization did not want to be an obstacle." This produced laughter, but, indeed, in this setting, with these leaders who shared my motivation, it was the greatest compliment ever paid me.

17

VPI-SU CONSUMER AFFAIRS OFFICE

My service in the governor's office was challenging and stimulating, almost indescribably so. I was right there in Richmond next to the seat of power, and I was aware of basically everything going on in the Commonwealth. Everything began and ended right there. It was a marvelous time for me.

I worked for Linwood Holton, a man I admired greatly. He will go down in history as one of the finest governors of the Commonwealth. He was the first governor of all the people of Virginia. His "New Dominion" approach will be discussed and praised one hundred years from now.

His administration was coming to an end, and, in Virginia, the governor could not succeed himself. Virginia Polytechnic Institute and State University (VPI-SU) officials and I had talked for several months about me going there to initiate programs for those not currently being reached by the university. Holton was aware of these talks and supported them. Officials at VPI wanted me to begin during the fall semester rather than wait until the administration ended the following January.

Holton agreed to this with the stipulation that I be allowed to continue my work with him until the actual end of the administration. The university agreed, stating that VPI would be proud to have one of its staff members on loan to the governor of Virginia.

In September 1973, I became a part of Virginia's land-grant institution as associate director of continuing education. I shall always have a great love for Virginia Polytechnic Institute and State University.

I began my VPI career of 2.5 days per week at the university and 2.5 each week in Richmond with the governor. The weekends always belonged to the governor with speeches to NAACP chapters, urban and rural Black churches, and social clubs.

It wasn't until after starting work in Blacksburg that I discovered the real restrictions of my new job. As special assistant to Linwood Holton, I had freedom of movement, involvement in mediating racial, prison, and consumer issues, and the ability to make a real difference in the lives of citizens who desperately needed an action-oriented approach. VPI did not see itself as a base from which these types of activities could originate. Instead, I was to plan conferences, determine how many people would need room accommodations, how many would eat breakfast, lunch, or whatever. I was expected to be an event planner, nothing more.

This was not what I expected. I became despondent. Going to Richmond was something to which I looked forward even though my family had moved to Blacksburg. Victoria had entered the university as a freshman, and Allen was attending the local high school.

My frustration heightened when a letter came from the Portsmouth Police Department asking that I help to kick off its attempt to recruit more minority policemen. I was asked to address chiefs of police from Hampton, Norfolk, and Newport News, emphasizing Portsmouth's open-door policy. This gave the project impetus from the highest office in the Commonwealth, the governor's office.

However, the date scheduled by the Portsmouth Police Department was set for one of the days I was to be at VPI rather than at the state capitol. I accepted the invitation anyway. I thought this was outreach and that the university would be willing for me to offer my services. I was wrong. The university was very much opposed to me using one of its days for this or any other purpose.

I felt I had been struggling so long to change this type of attitudinal behavior on the part of high-ranking police officials that I had to participate. I informed everyone from the president down to my immediate supervisor that I had to go. Reluctantly, they gave permission. It was obvious they were unhappy. So was I.

Looking back on the agreement that took me to Blacksburg, there simply was a lack of real communication. I thought that audiences not currently reached by the university meant Blacks, Hispanics, Native Americans, and disadvantaged Whites and that I would use my skills in mediating, negotiating, and using sociological insights to assist those who continued to need help. The university was adamant in what it wanted—a person to set up conferences.

Johnnie, as usual, understood and advised me. "Either settle into this position and be satisfied or find another that gives you satisfaction," she said. She told me that she and the children would support my decision.

During this period, I was in touch with Governor Robert Ray of Iowa, a Republican in the mold of Linwood Holton. Ray told me that he would like to talk with Johnnie and me. He said that he would soon be in Washington and that a date would be forwarded to see if I would be willing to meet with him. A few days later one of his aides called and told me that Ray would be in Washington in November. I offered to pick them up at Washington National Airport. We did this on a cold Sunday evening after driving five hours across the state. Ray, Johnnie, his wife, and I talked for some four or five hours and parted with the assurance that Ray would soon be back in touch. He asked us to visit Des Moines. We believed that I would join him at the state capitol in Des Moines as a mediator/negotiator in various phases of state governmental activities.

The very next day, one of my secretaries in Richmond called me at VPI to tell me that a job description had arrived stating that Commissioner Walter E. Washington was seeking a person to head a new department he was creating, the District of Columbia Office of Consumer Affairs. From the way it read, she said she thought I would be perfect for the position.

When I got to work in Richmond the following Wednesday, I studied the announcement thoroughly. I decided to apply. A few days later I received a call asking if I would come for an interview. The big question centered on just how I would operate, whether I would go charging off every time it was reported that a violation had taken place or would I take into consideration all or both sides of a dispute and render fair decisions. It brought me right back to the mediating and negotiating posture I had always taken. I had not heard anything from Ray in over a month. My calls to him found the governor away from the office or in conference.

On November 27, 1973, Washington officials announced that I would be going to Washington to serve as that city's first director of consumer affairs. My duties would begin on December 3. Holton explained the situation to the president at VPI, who was very understanding. He also indicated to Washington that he needed me for at least 2.5 days per week until the end of his administration in January. Washington agreed to this.

Ray did call me back to offer me the job, but not until after I had committed to the job in the District of Columbia. He apologized and explained that he had become so busy he had gotten behind in personnel matters.

18

BALANCING TIME IN WASHINGTON, D.C.

The last day of November 1973, I left VPI in order to begin my duties in Washington. I now understand I went to a college campus too soon after having served in the governor's office. I admit that I had heard what I wanted to hear about my VPI job description. I thought it was about helping Blacks, women, and other minorities, not deciding how many chairs to set up per row for a conference. I respected and admired Virginia Tech's president, T. Marshall Hahn, his support of diversity, and his vision for the future. I hoped that, at another point in my life, I would return to the beautiful campus as a lecturer in the area of human relations or a related field.

I arrived in Washington on a day that was cold, dark, and dreary. I entered the building that was to become the Office of Consumer Affairs. It, too, was cold, dark, and dreary. The District of Columbia government was renting it but using it for storage. One employee, a telephone operator, was on duty in the only heated room. In spite of the venetian blinds falling from the windows, layers of dust, dilapidated furniture, and the drabness and gloominess of the facility, I began to visualize what the place could be.

I called Catherine Shelton, who had worked closely with me in the governor's office and had become a very good friend of the family, not realizing what was in store for us. Catherine agreed to become my administrative assistant. She moved her family to Northern Virginia. We worked together to get the office in shape and began to hire staff while handling consumer complaints. We attempted to be a true equal employment agency, hiring through the personnel department Blacks, Hispanics, and females as well as Whites.

Things began to take shape. We planned an investigative department and an education component. The office became brighter, more comfortable for staff and those consumers, businesspeople, and governmental people who would come to the office. My philosophy was that when people walked into the office, regardless of socioeconomic status, they should find an efficient, friendly, bright, and cheerful atmosphere awaiting them. All repairs and improvements were given approval by the District of Columbia government.

The office held its official opening in January 1974, still a bit shy of staff and chairs but prepared to do business. Our neighbors on the block, consumer advocates, businesspeople, and the curious came for the ribbon cutting. Mayor Washington gave us our charge and cut the ribbon. On this cold January day, the female minister who offered the invocation encouraged us to love each other.

In 1973–74, Washington, D.C., was embroiled in the Watergate and post-Watergate controversies. Everything and everyone were suspect. Investigative reporting was the order of the day. Fed by the flames started by those who wished to see the marketplace as a battleground, I was targeted with complaints. I could do nothing right and was constantly criticized by consumer advocates. They wanted me to start lawsuits and court cases.

Using education, investigation, and mediation, I felt we were moving in the right direction. Of course, over time, this would have led to court cases. I requested that the D.C. government do both in-house and independent evaluations of the office to determine its effectiveness. This was done, and both assessments proved to be positive.

Local consumer groups and I began to hold strategy sessions to determine how to approach business concerns to bring about change. We met in the boardrooms of some of the most powerful people in Washington. Black consumers spoke for themselves and could see change coming. These actions surprised my detractors.

In 1975, the other so-called advocates challenged me to come to a meeting to answer questions about my style. This I had done before, and I knew I would be the loser because it would be attack, attack, attack on their part and in their ball park. Instead of responding to their invitation, I issued one of my own, stating that if they would choose any two of their representatives, I would be happy to meet and debate them on any television station in Washington. Copies of my letter went to every television station and newspaper in Washington.

This move surprised my critics. It seemed almost as if they had disappeared. They did not respond, nor did the media make a move right away. A secret paper was circulated from my critics, those who called themselves consumer advocates, suggesting that they should not respond to my challenge to debate on television because this would give me a forum and that, since I was a real windbag, I would monopolize the time available. One of the stations picked up my challenge, and my opponents could not back out. It was two of them pitted against me. My philosophy prevailed as I listened to them argue between themselves. I had a policy. They did not have one they could agree upon. I knew my philosophy had won.

I had shown that the marketplace does not necessarily have to be a place of constant confrontation but rather could be one where men and women of goodwill iron out their differences to the mutual benefit of all, that businesspeople should be able to attempt to make a legitimate profit, that consumers had the right to goods and services equal to the prices they paid, and both working together must constantly be vigilant as they guard against those who would tilt the scales in either direction. All the things I had come to Washington to do had come into being. I had helped needy consumers to identify ways in which to help themselves. I had established a highly efficient office. I had served the people of Washington and in doing so helped Walter Edward Washington to become the first Black elected mayor of the District of Columbia.

It may have been modest, but it was the beginning of a new way of thinking.

19

KENYA

In February 1975, while working at the Washington Consumer Affairs Office, I received a call from the White House. As a former assistant to a Republican governor, I was no stranger to calls of this nature, but I did wonder what this caller from the Ford administration had on his mind.

The caller explained that President Gerald Ford was seeking African Americans who might be interested in international positions. "You've been involved in government at the local, state, and national levels—would you be interested?" I immediately said yes.

"Then, we'll be back in touch with you," he said.

I didn't give this much thought until a few months later, when I received another call asking me to meet with Peace Corps officials. A director's position would become open in a few months in Jamaica, and the Peace Corps caller asked if I would be interested in it.

Again, I said yes. It was September 1975 before I heard more. I bought books and maps and other materials to learn about Jamaica, but just before Thanksgiving, I was called to the Peace Corps office. There I was told that the White House wanted me to go not to Jamaica but to Kenya. I needed to be ready by February 1976. What a surprise.

"Are they crazy?" my wife said. "It's Thanksgiving, then it will be Christmas. There is no way we can be ready by February." It helped when we learned that our training would start in February and we would actually leave for Nairobi in April.

With a lot of hard work and help from friends, we got ready. When we'd left Roanoke to go to work for Holton in Richmond, we had found renters for our home in Roanoke. Now, we decided to sell it. Luckily for us, our renters wanted to buy it. That took care of one part of our life.

Victoria was at Virginia Tech, and Allen was a senior at Herndon (Virginia) High School. Johnnie and I decided we would go on to Kenya and let the children come when the school term ended. My Jaycee buddy Bill Poff and his wife, Mag, would see to it that the children functioned well until we were together again as a family. Poff was a leading attorney in Roanoke, and Mag was a writer for the *Roanoke World-News*. I loved them both. They were our very best friends, and we trusted them with our children. The most important part of our lives was organized for this adventure to take place.

After going through training, we were off to Kenya and, unknown to us at the time, to years of involvement with other African countries. Kenya was the second-largest post in all of the Peace Corps, with 300 volunteers and trainees. Only the Philippines, with 375, had more.

The culture shock began when we entered the country. For the first time I was a member of the majority. Bank tellers, police, salespeople, the country's president, members of parliament—all were Black. So were all the people in advertising, television, magazines, and billboards.

Nairobi's elevation is 5,800 feet, more than a mile high. That is high enough to affect cooking, especially baking. The lack of oxygen is said to be an advantage for training champion Kenyan runners. Allen's strongest sensory memory of Kenya, more than forty years later, is of the air. He said it was somehow brighter. The sky seemed clearer and bluer. There were mountains in the distance, and we were all amazed at the thousands of stars visible at night. By day, there were monkeys everywhere. We saw them swipe salt shakers from outdoor diners and run with them.

The weather was wonderful, much like southern California, with temperatures usually in the 70s with low humidity, allowing a year-round growing season. We never had to wear coats. The city was bathed in green all the time, with lush, ever-blooming, bright flowers flourishing everywhere. The city's nickname is "The Green City in the Sun" with good reason.

Like American cities, Nairobi featured skyscrapers, buses, and crowds. Most people wore Western clothing, but there were also many wearing kitenge cloth, well-known African cotton print fabrics decorated with Swahili proverbs on the borders. We noticed that Kenyans took care to be clean and wore the best that they had. Swahili is one of the easiest African languages for English speakers, and we learned enough to get by. For example, *bwana* means "sir" or "boss"; *mzee* is a respectful term for an old, wise man; and *hakuna matata* means "no worries."

We lived outside Nairobi in an international community within a compound with high fences. The windows were louvered, the doors were chained, and radio contact was maintained with the U.S. embassy. Foreign residents were often targeted for break-ins and robberies. Our home was a multilevel house with a view of a river, unheated except for a fireplace. There was no television, but we did have a refrigerator and washer and dryer. Johnnie shopped for fresh food every day. I missed Sunday football. It helped to get the Roanoke paper with the scores even three weeks late.

We were expected to hire Kenyans to help in our home: a cook; a driver; a *shamba* man, or gardener; and an *askari,* or guard. This helped the local economy. For one thing, they needed money to pay school fees for their children. All of them lived on our family's compound, and we were responsible for them.

The cook prepared our meals and also cleaned the house and even ironed. We had goat, beef, lamb, and pork with rice or cooked cornmeal mush called *ugali.* Beans and barbeque were popular. Apples were expensive and scarce, but bananas and passion fruit were plentiful. At first, I would take our cook's three-year-old son to town with me if it were to be a short trip, but I was criticized for spoiling him. I gave him candy, though. It upset me when the American families celebrated Halloween and left out the Kenyan children.

Most Americans in Nairobi had drivers because cars travel in the left lane, like in the United Kingdom, and drivers were aggressive. In addition, there were complicated roundabouts and few traffic controls plus additional political pressure: an American driver who caused an accident could be part of an international incident. Johnnie said she was afraid to drive there.

Our *shamba* man took care of flowers and ornamental plants but also tended a two-acre garden year-round to partially meet our food needs. He harvested a variety of edible plants, from collard greens to bananas.

Our *askari* was a small man from a warrior tribe, armed with a machete. There weren't guns to fear, but Panga-panga gangs also armed with machetes existed, and wild dogs ran in packs. Idi Amin was president of neighboring Uganda at the time, and Victoria had nightmares about him.

To go to town, we could walk up the hill and, for a small fee, catch a small car, a *matatue,* to the city. Some riders carried chickens on board with them. We soon learned that the ride was dangerous. Once our *matatue* turned a corner on two wheels. Some crashed and turned over. Once we saw a dead body by the road on the way to town; it was still there on the way back.

I went to the rural areas, "upcountry," about thirteen days each month. I was a high-ranking government official and moved in the circles of high officials of Kenya and America as well as other foreign governments, but also with the people of rural villages. Some days I was a "father," an educator, a counselor, even a college president in this challenging job.

I truly fell in love with the Kenyan people. I tried to learn as much about the culture as I could. As part of that effort, I endeavored to eat all the foods offered me. The most difficult was goat, killed and cooked in front of me, but I did it. I really enjoyed their spicy foods and mangos. When the embassies held big parties and they wanted the common people to attend, they came to me because I was well known among the people. I was active in a number of organizations, including the Jaycees and other groups that supported the handicapped. I was visible in my community and had friends and acquaintances in outlying areas.

My day began before 8:00 a.m., when our driver took me to work in Nairobi. I stayed in the office until 1:00 p.m., then he came to pick me up and take me home for lunch until 2:00 p.m., then back to work. Everything closed at 5:00 p.m. An evening out in Kenya could include a meal at a restaurant, usually steak for me with spicy side dishes. We could watch a first-release movie in English or go to the National Theater for live entertainment. The Norfolk Hotel was a British hangout at that time, and it had a teatime daily.

We occasionally went sightseeing. Johnnie and I visited Nyeri, a city established by the British in the Central Highlands. We walked to the sign showing the location of the equator. We experienced the grandeur of Mount Kilimanjaro from a distance.

It was new and exciting to be part of this era of development in Africa. My work with the developmentally disabled served me well because Kenya was just beginning on a large scale to address the issues surrounding disabilities. Special-education teachers were being trained.

I located the Kenya Jaycees and joined. In the United States, I was named a Junior Chamber International Senator and Ambassador. This gave me the experience and status to be welcomed by the young Jaycee organization. Kenya's Jaycees group was basically Indian businessmen and -women under the age of forty. I became a leader in the organization. The Jaycees began to establish programs for the developmentally disabled by providing money to build schools. I had become a member of the Kenya Society for the Mentally Handicapped, and as a result of my Jaycee involvement, I married the two organizations in Kenya.

However, my first responsibility was to the Peace Corps' early-attrition problem. When I arrived, early attrition was approximately 20 percent, and I had to address this issue. I saw the need for the Peace Corps staff to provide more support to the volunteers in Kenya. Therefore, I put in place the following activities:

1. Two all-volunteer conferences to be held per year.
2. Two volunteer sector meetings to be held per year.
3. A volunteer advisory committee.
4. Extending office hours to include Saturdays 9:00–noon in the Peace Corps office in Nairobi so volunteers could have more time with staff.
5. As director, I would visit each volunteer at least once per year.
6. Each assistant Peace Corps director would visit each volunteer in his/her sector once per year.

In every aspect of the programming in Kenya, I began to refer to us as a "family," with me being the father. The volunteers began calling me "Dad." The volunteers felt more connected to each other, all three hundred, to work with Kenyans, to teach and learn to help bring about a better quality of life for Kenyans.

It was important to realize that these volunteers were alone, that is to say, they were the only American in the areas where they worked. I met every incoming volunteer at the airport as they arrived. There were fewer than ten Black volunteers in the group of three hundred working with a Black population, some interacting with Black people for the first time. We had a bedroom in our home set aside for Peace Corps volunteers, especially those who were physically ill or homesick. Sometimes they needed someone to talk to, and during their two-year tour they occasionally needed to talk to someone who understood American jokes, or to just visit. Sometimes people were simply not a good match. One tough Japanese American doctor left, saying: "They don't need me. I'm leaving."

It was a varied group. For example, we had teachers, nurses, rich kids from California, government planners, doctors, engineers, and a cowboy from Montana who helped Kenyans learn to raise cows more efficiently.

When volunteers left early, American dollars that were paid for training were wasted and Kenya, the host country, had not been served. Technically, they weren't really volunteering, even though Kenya provided housing. The American government paid a small monthly salary and held back enough to give them a lump sum at the end of their two years. I promoted awareness that after completing the two years they also had work experience to offer employers as well as documented capability to adapt to a foreign culture and language. After a while sectors began working together for a common purpose. The sectors were education, agriculture, nursing (health), rural and urban development, engineering, and entrepreneurship. Each sector was headed by an assistant Peace Corps director educated in that particular field.

One of the ideas to help my volunteers complete their term was to host conferences to bring us all together. I was challenged by a coworker to provide "proof that you really are God—get Lillian Carter to speak to our workers." Lillian Carter was most famous as the mother of President Jimmy Carter, but she was famous in her own right as a nurse and political activist. She served in the Peace Corps in India beginning at age sixty-eight. I accepted the challenge and sent her a request to speak. I was told that she was so surprised to get my invitation that she nearly dropped her false teeth. She agreed to speak by phone. After a dinner during a Peace Corps Conference in Nairobi in the spring of 1978, I silenced the volunteers as the phone rang. They were surprised and listened to the speaker-phone: "The White House is calling . . ." Then Mrs. Carter spoke about her experiences and how important Peace Corps workers were. Her speech was inspirational to dozens of young people far from home.

Volunteers began to feel they had more voice in what they were doing. They began to appreciate staff more. No longer did they feel they were thrown into a different culture and forgotten about. We were a Peace Corps family working in unison to bring about development for Kenya and friendship for America. These Peace Corps volunteers were some of the finest people of all ages I have ever met. With the support of Mrs. Carter and others and the many smaller tweaks in the system, our attrition problem began to clear up.

In early June 1976, Peace Corps officials had asked me to return to Washington for a Peace Corps conference. Fortunately, this was the time Allen was graduating from Herndon High School, and we were able to attend. Victoria was also completing her year at Virginia Tech. My wife traveled with me, and we packed them up to return to Kenya with us. They were great unpaid staff for over a year. They interacted well with the volunteers, many of whom were kids from universities. Often, they picked up on concerns I needed to deal with that otherwise might have been delayed or never realized.

There were incidents of cultural transition for both our grown children when they arrived. Allen's first realization of being in the majority came as he watched from a second-floor balcony of the Norfolk Hotel and saw throngs of people below going back and forth, to work or to shop. The sea of Black faces impressed him. At first, because of the elevation, Victoria and Allen were often out of breath. Victoria, at twenty-one, did not like the cook's version of what we called "British" food: bland potatoes and green beans and unseasoned collard greens. Johnnie took matters in hand and taught the cook to prepare soul food for our meals. Victoria was also uncomfortable with the male cook cleaning her room. She declined his help and did it herself.

We were all very involved in the culture of Kenya. Allen taught basketball to Kenyan girls. He had been a member of his high school varsity basketball team. He also played bassoon with the Nairobi Symphony Orchestra and was part of international musical casts. West African Highlife music was popular at the time, a style that involved intricate African rhythms, multiple guitars, and jazz horns. Allen called it Hawaiian music with an African sound. Victoria was a dancer and starred in productions by the Kenya National Theater. She taught dance to young Kenyan women with intellectual and developmental disabilities at Treeside School. Johnnie started a school in one of the villages. She played the harp and also participated in a range of educational projects in the American Women's Association in the international community.

Victoria was active upcountry and joined with some local women to travel to the Rift Valley. She did not completely understand Swahili, but the lessons provided by Peace Corps trainers were enough for her to understand that they were going to a Maasai family's home for the weekend for some sort of festival. Once there, she found herself a guest in a hut made of mud and cow dung. The family, their guests, and all the animals gathered in the hut to sleep.

The next day, she watched the women dance but didn't join in because she didn't know the steps. She learned later that the women assumed that because she was Black, she had left and gone to Britain and had forgotten the traditional ways before her return. As the activity began, a horn containing a blood-and-milk mixture was passed around, and each woman drank. When she realized that the women were preparing for the circumcision of several young girls, she slipped away. As she tried to gather her wits, she returned to bear witness and watched one girl writhe and cry. Later, she learned that the girl would likely be ostracized and was told she'd not get a good husband. Female genitalia mutilation in Kenya has been banned since 2011 with both successes and failures.

As I was going out the door bound for Kenya, some official had whispered in my ear: "You also supervise seven volunteers in Seychelles." This is an island 1,300 miles off the coast of Kenya and a former British colony. My family and I were there in 1976 when the Union Jack came down and the Republic of Seychelles flag went up. It is a beautiful island, located in the deep-blue water of the Indian Ocean. Tourism is important there; the island is a famous honeymoon destination. I visited the nation several times and lobbied for the residents and volunteers to have their own Peace Corps director, which has since happened.

We watched a powerful dance, the Moutya, created by enslaved African people with lyrics from Seychelles Creole. It depicts the anger and misery felt by the enslaved men and women and is always performed in the open air. A prominent Seychellois historian, Norbert Salomon, explained the origin of the dance: "Whilst the White European masters danced in their great halls, the slaves created their own dance to declare their suffering."

In my time in Kenya, I was active with the Jaycees, the Kenya Society for the Mentally Handicapped, and worked with its chairman, Mr. O. A. Menya, his wife, and other members of the organization: Christine Kenyatta, head of special education for the Ministry of Education and the daughter of Jomo Kenyatta, the late president of Kenya; Catherine Abilla; ministry officials; parents; and special-needs children and adults. Working with the Jaycees, I helped to bring into being the Kenya Special Olympics.

President Kennedy appointed Sargent Shriver as the first director of the Peace Corps. Shriver was also a former U.S. ambassador to France, and with his wife, Eunice Kennedy Shriver, he visited us in Kenya. She was not feeling well and came to Kenya for some rest. I'm afraid she did not get very much. The American ambassador put me in charge of the Shrivers, and I knew she wanted to focus on those with special needs. Our Peace Corps program centered on the endeavors in which she was interested. She also attended meetings of the Society for the Mentally Handicapped. The Shrivers were very gracious and really helped us strengthen the Kenyan programs. When I left Kenya in 1979 at the conclusion of my three-year Peace Corps tour, I left part of my heart there. My efforts to lower the 20 percent early-attrition rate of the Kenyan Peace Corps had been successful; it had fallen to 5 percent. It felt as if we had made a difference in educating the young people, building houses, drilling wells, and preventing disease. I had been well received by the people, and many wanted me to stay. They told me that I was a Kenyan. I told them I could help them more back in the States because now I better knew their needs.

I was grateful for the comments of appreciation offered for my work in Kenya. Shanti Chauhan, Kenya Jaycees immediate past chairman, described the reasons for the Kenya Jaycee Distinguished Service Award: "Jaycees Senator/Ambassador Bill Robertson traveled around the country speaking before Jaycee chapters causing increased interest and membership, helped bring about a sister chapter relationship between Kisumu and Roanoke, assisted in developing the 1979 theme, 'Handicapped Children Our Concern,' championed the cause of handicapped children, brought into being the first chapter of Black Kenyan Jaycees, assisted in gaining governmental support, served as an inspiration to all Kenyans, regardless of race, creed, colour, sex to form bonds of friendship, and brotherhood." Mrs. M. J. Menya, chief executive officer of the Kenya National Council of Social Service, wrote to Secretary of Defense Caspar Weinberger: "Through Bill's assistance, we have progressed a great deal through Treeside School, teacher training, strengthening of our organization, and creation of Kenyan Special Olympics."

Mr. Wilbert J. LeMelle, U.S. ambassador to Kenya, sent a telegram to Washington that detailed the Peace Corps influence: "I doubt that there is any Peace Corps program anywhere so well appreciated as Peace Corps Kenya's projects of aid for the handicapped. The Peace Corps' ability to provide qualified volunteers in this field has earned the PC well-deserved public recognition and gratitude. Washington should be extremely proud of this work, the success of which has been in good measure due to the efforts of outgoing Peace Corps Director Bill Robertson, who can leave Nairobi with a true sense of a job well done, which has reflected credit upon himself, the Peace Corps, and the American Government."

Partly because of my Peace Corps work, partly due to Camp Virginia Jaycee and teacher integration, in 1976 I was named as a recipient of the Bicentennial Award of the National Education Association (NEA), one of approximately twenty-four people in the country to receive the award. This awards program was created to honor people who have made significant contributions to the NEA Bicentennial theme, "A Declaration of Interdependence: Education for a Global Community." I was flattered and humbled by this recognition, but I was not able to be present for the ceremony in Miami in June 1976 for I was on the other side of the world.

20

PEOPLE-TO-PEOPLE PROGRAMMING

I was lonely after returning home from Kenya to Reston, Virginia. I missed the people of Kenya. My mother passed away in 1980. I think she was happy during her later years, at least until she became sick. She had been ill for months before her death.

I had never done anything without my mamma. When I needed to make a major decision, she would tell me to put my thoughts in writing or sit down at the table and think about things. I found myself reaching for the phone to call her even after she was gone. I missed her so much. I regretted that we did not take her to Kenya with us.

I missed Kenya, too. There were two undertakings regarding Kenya still left in my heart. First, I wanted to come up with a way in which Johnnie and I could stay involved with the people and programs there and, at the same time, provide the people of Reston, our new community, an opportunity to meet and know the people of Kenya. In a book by Laverne Gill, *Reston's African American Legacy,* she summed up our motivation: "They wanted to do something for both of their loves, their new hometown of Reston and the people of Kenya."

The people-to-people programs initiated by President Dwight D. Eisenhower in 1956 came to mind. International student exchanges and Sister

Cities International were products of the same philosophy. These programs were created as an alternative to war, a means for citizen diplomacy through cultural exchanges.

Earlier, my native city of Roanoke called upon me to find a city in Kenya that would serve as its sister city. I was able to do this by pairing Kisumu, Kenya, with Roanoke. The towns had commonalities: they were both railroad towns and were located near broad valleys, Kisumu in the Rift Valley and Roanoke in the Roanoke Valley. Both towns formed Sister City committees and developed a strong people-to-people relationship. Roanoke has seven sister cities, and Kisumu is still one of them.

With this in mind, I sought to develop a people-to-people Sister City program between Reston and a city in Kenya. I contacted Reston Black Focus and the Reston Community Association to determine interest in the project. There were those in Reston who voiced disapproval of linking with an African city. They expressed the idea that a Scandinavian city would be more appropriate.

However, there was enough support to continue the project. I contacted officials in Nyeri to assess their interest, which was high. Contact was made with Sister Cities International, and the twinning was made official in 1981.

The Sister City partnership brought together a broad cross-section of Restonians and Nyerians. Schoolchildren became pen pals with students in a foreign land. The Reston Lions Club formed a relationship with its Kenyan counterpart. A church got a sister church. The Reston Boy Scout troop even partnered with a troop in Nyeri. The Nyeri City Council set aside unused land and created "Reston Park." Reston Community Association secured grant funding to build a special-education facility.

We brought two special-education teachers from Nyeri to Camp Virginia Jaycee via Reston. The teachers trained at the camp and learned best practices in outdoor recreation and educational camping during the summer of 1981. Lesson plans and curricula were developed for use in Kenyan classrooms. They taught our special-needs campers "*shamba* work," agricultural techniques or simply how to garden. They communicated the magic of seeing plants grow and harvested vegetables and used them in camp meals. In Kenya, every person has to carry his or her own weight. Therefore, family members with special needs work in the fields. We learned that much more is expected of them in Kenya than here in the United States. The Kenyan teachers thought we coddled our special-needs population. On weekends, the teachers came to Reston to live with families and speak in their schools and churches.

In 1983, another pair of Kenyan special-education teachers, Susan Karugu and Agnes Peter, made the fifteen-hour flight to Virginia and immediately began training at Camp Virginia Jaycee. They learned every facet of camp life, especially administration of the camp, food services, and new recreational activities.

"We're going to start a camp for the mentally retarded . . . it's never been done before in our country," Mrs. Peter said. The women said mentally retarded children everywhere deserve the same things nonhandicapped children do: love, patience, and dedication.

"We also learned the different types of ball you play here. In Kenya we only throw the softball. We play rounders, the English version of baseball. We will take back the knowledge of your games."

The teacher exchange program won an award from the Peace Corps for fostering the concept of peace and friendship and one from the National Organization on Disability for promoting the Decade of the Disabled. The project also won a presidential award from the President's Committee on Mental Retardation.

Restonians visited Kenya. I accompanied a group of Reston residents to Kenya, where they met Christine Kenyatta and the vice president of the country, Mwai Kibaki, and visited the special-education teachers who had come to Virginia.

The program expanded to the point that we also brought special-education teachers from Sierra Leone and Black special-education teachers from South Africa. During a period of roughly ten years, until the program ended in 1990, we brought thirty educators together to train them to establish similar educational programs and adapt them to the needs of their students.

It truly was an extraordinary two-way development effort. They learned from us, and we from them. This was the first Sister City program in Fairfax County, Virginia, and it earned multiple awards and recognition. Fairfax County saluted our work, as did then Virginia governor Chuck Robb. The Peace Corps and the President's Committee on Mental Retardation applauded our efforts to expand opportunities for the mentally disabled. In 1986, the Reston/Nyeri partnership won five first-place awards from Sister Cities International.

The editors and staff of the *Reston Times* select a Citizen of the Year annually. In 1989, they chose me, citing accolades for my work with the Reston/Nyeri Sister City program. They offered this confirmation of progress:

"When Robertson started working to promote special education in Kenya, that nation had only three schools for mentally handicapped students. Today it has 85." The program had many friends, and it ran on their goodwill and donations. The people of Reston gave me a lot of leeway to run the program and provided strong support. One of the greatest rewards for me is the shared sense of community between Reston and Nyeri.

The second project bound by heartstrings attached to Kenya turned out to be lengthier and even more complex. When I was helping to organize the Special Olympics, one of the volunteer coaches, Patrick Wanyama, spoke to me about his nephew, Francis Maloba. Francis was about sixteen years old when Patrick introduced us. Francis dreamed of becoming a doctor and working in the impoverished Kenyan backcountry near his hometown of Nyeri. He came from a more comfortable background than many young people in his country, but he could not afford to attend college abroad. I told him I would help him.

Francis's school operated on the British system of educational levels: "A" level was equivalent to our junior college, and "O" level corresponded to our twelfth grade. Francis had completed the "O" level. I advised him to complete the "A" level and carefully consider the decision to leave his home and family. This would give him another year or two at home and perhaps strengthen him to help him to be able to leave if that was still his desire. He completed the "A" level, still determined to follow his dream.

The Sister City program made it possible for him to come to the United States. Funding was secured from the United States Agency for International Development. Churches in Reston, including the Martin Luther King Jr. Church, the Presbyterian Church, and St. Thomas a Becket Catholic Church, donated to the cause, and so did the Eisenhower International Classic, a charity that benefits Sister Cities International.

Francis had a scholarship of one thousand dollars for five years and enrolled in St. Paul's College in Lawrenceburg, where the fees were seven thousand to ten thousand dollars per year. He lived with us during school breaks and worked at Camp Virginia Jaycee during the summers. Community members generously contributed and got him through undergraduate school.

Francis was a wonderful ambassador. He worked hard in his studies and found time to speak in classrooms, churches, and living rooms to correct misconceptions on both sides of the Atlantic. He thoughtfully explained that Africa was not the primitive place depicted in movies and added his own surprise at discovering that there were homeless people in the United States. "In Kenya, people think everyone in the U.S. is rich," he said.

He was smart, polite, and soft-spoken. His athletic ability earned him a place on the St. Paul's football team as a kicker. One season, his team was behind 55–0 against Norfolk State. By the fourth quarter, it seemed apparent that St. Paul's was not even going to score. On a fourth-down play near the end of the game, Francis was sent in to kick a 38-yard field goal. We were so proud when he made it. St. Paul's had scored!

We were even prouder when, after transferring to Virginia Commonwealth University in Richmond, Francis graduated with a bachelor of science degree in pre-med and biology. He then returned home for two years to reacquaint himself with family and the reason he wanted to be a doctor in the first place. "It made me stronger and much more motivated," he said upon returning.

Now he was ready for medical school. He applied to school after school, and we tried to help, but it seemed that we were going around and around with no progress. Nothing came of our efforts. Finally, on the last day of Camp Virginia Jaycee for the season, good news arrived. He had been accepted at Howard University College of Medicine. It was announced at the big party attended by campers and counselors, and they celebrated with him. How exciting that one of their own was going to medical school.

Howard University was going to cost more than double the fees required for undergraduate school, upward of thirty thousand dollars per year. Even the generous people of Reston could not be expected to fund such an amount. This was a serious obstacle.

Here is where the Almighty once again became obvious in my life and in the lives of those I cared about. Years ago, I was in a group of eight favorite students of my friend and professor Mrs. Othello Harris-Jefferson. All of us had been asked to help with her affairs. I had outlived the other seven students and was able to take care of the last arrangements when Mrs. Jefferson's sister passed away. Then, when Mrs. Jefferson died, I completed the things she had asked me to do and planned her memorial service and burial. In her will, she left Bluefield State College the largest endowment an individual had ever bestowed. Shockingly, she also left me a large amount of money. I had never spent it or even spoken of it. This was a cause that I believed Mrs. Jefferson would be pleased to support, so I chose to use that money to pay the medical school tuition for Francis Maloba. It was my gift to Kenya.

We were very close to helping this young man fulfill his personal dream and our joint goal of providing an indigenous doctor for the rural area near Nyeri. He graduated from Howard University but barely missed scoring high enough on the medical boards after repeated attempts.

I had often cautioned him to not get involved with an American girl as I suspected she would not want to leave the United States and live in Kenya, thus keeping him from practicing medicine there. When he called to let me know he was serious about a wonderful girl, he quickly added, "Mkubwa, wise man, don't worry, she is Kenyan." They were married and now have a family.

In 2010, Francis nominated me for a "We Deliver Award." He wrote in his nomination:

> As a teenager, I was intimidated to meet a founder of the Special Olympics in Kenya, but was disarmed by his unassuming nature and his strong desire and interest that I pursue my goal of becoming a medical doctor. . . . He said he was going to help. I thought he was just being nice given the number of responsibilities he had on his plate. Where would he find time to fit me in? . . . I knew he wasn't going to call or write. So, I went back to my boarding high school and forgot about it until I received college application forms from the United States, a year and a half later, courtesy of Mr. Robertson. No, he didn't forget and years later on my path to medical school, I found out why. Mr. Robertson's commitment was of the type that impacted whole communities. . . . I wasn't too small or too insignificant to forget. In the bigger picture, I mattered. He therefore saw to it that I received my education.
>
> I never expected that I would pursue medicine and public health in the United States and be in a position to affect livelihoods of two continents. Did Mr. Robertson deliver? Yes, and even better than a mailman because he delivers on Sundays as well.

Francis went on to graduate in administration from George Washington University and is currently working in the Washington, D.C., area. His life is a three-decades-long success story that we were all honored to be involved with.

Our hope is that, as he gets older, he will go back to Kenya and help his people even more.

21

STATE DEPARTMENT

I had known Secretary of Defense Caspar Weinberger since my days on the President's Committee on Mental Retardation some dozen years before, so when there was a vacancy at the State Department that matched my qualifications, he evidently thought of me and shared my information with Secretary of State George P. Shultz. I was appointed as the deputy assistant secretary of state for African affairs by President Ronald Reagan. I rotated in two-week intervals: two weeks traveling to African countries, learning and conducting business with appreciation of the differences between many governments, then returning home to Reston for two weeks. My primary responsibilities were to help Africans with business issues, to report human rights violations in each country, to work toward dismantling apartheid, to handle other State Department priorities as they arose, to assess needs, to get donations delivered through customs and in spite of transportation concerns, and to write seemingly endless reports. I worked out of the U.S. embassy in each country.

When asked how a "Bobby Kennedy Democrat" transitioned to a "Linwood Holton Republican" and then to work for President Ronald Reagan, I answer simply that my work with his administration allowed me to continue the efforts that brought me so much satisfaction. There were two particular facets of my work that I considered most important. First, I was able to continue problem solving with people-to-people approaches, as advocated earlier by President Eisenhower. This brought me high praise from President Reagan's secretary of state, George Shultz. Second, President Reagan and I shared the same goal in approaching South Africa's apartheid, undoubtedly for different reasons, but with the same end game: avoiding economic sanctions. I understood that the Reagan administration was labeled "racist," but nevertheless, I felt I could make a positive difference in the lives of Black people in the United States and abroad. I was excited to begin this work and continue my firsthand interactions with the peoples of Africa.

Africa still conjures up many misconceptions and stereotypes. Too many of us think of Africa as being one big monolithic country. Africa is often imagined as that place where lions and other wild animals walk through villages and cities. These concepts must be tackled and changed in such a way that people understand that sub-Saharan Africa is composed of fifty-four countries with many different languages, tribes, and cultures. Certainly, animals do not stalk the streets of African cities.

My African friends told me that it really upset them to find that a great many of them are able to tell us the name of the president of the United States and name members of the cabinet, to know the geography of our country, but we cannot reciprocate. We do not know where African nations are located. We do not know the names of their countries' leaders.

In the mid- to late 1980s, my time in the State Department, the images of Africa in the minds of most Americans seemed to be those of starving children in Ethiopia and the cruelty taking place in South Africa. As I spoke to a variety of groups in this country, I strived to share that, in spite of a myriad of problems, Africa was alive, vibrant, filled with human and natural resources, and ready to take its place on the world's stage. I was excited about the potential for that part of the world and was awed at the diversity in both the landscapes and the people.

Africa is "The Mother Continent," so named because it is the oldest inhabited continent. People have lived there for hundreds of thousands of years, evolving into uncountable ethnic groups and developing an estimated two thousand languages.

The physical diversity of the land is almost beyond description. From an airplane window, I've viewed the desert ergs, the one-thousand-foot-high sand dunes of Algeria and Libya, along with the waterless prehistoric seabeds, the regs of the Sahara. In southern Libya, I saw one hundred miles of desert with not one plant that could take root. In contrast, I saw giant baobab trees in Senegal, eighty feet tall and said to be thousands of years old. I've seen the rapid desertification of the Sahel, drought and deforestation taking their toll. A nimble wild goat put on a brief show for me on the rocky "Roof of Africa," the craggy mountains of the Ethiopian Highlands formed by magma. In Tanzania, Mount Kilimanjaro—the tallest freestanding mountain in the world—can have snow at any time of the year, and glaciers sparkle nearby. The scene is again different on the rich grasslands of the Serengeti stretching from Kenya to Tanzania. I have watched the wind gently move the grasses from above, then seen the motion grow as millions of wildebeests and zebras and gazelles migrate in herds, trampling and fertilizing the grass to allow new growth. I have visited the Swahili Coast, where mangrove tree forests grow, and the rapidly declining rain forests on the Congo River basin, where plant life is so diverse that only one-tenth of the species have even been identified. Surrounding the Rift Valley, where I made my home in Kenya, are the African Great Lakes, seven lakes among the deepest and largest in the world. Farther south, the flowers and moss and ferns of Southern Africa's Cape Floral Region stretch as far as your eye, or even your binoculars, can see. Even farther south, a colony of penguins lives an hour from Cape Town in South Africa.

It is a vast land of opposites. Africa encompasses both glaciers and monsoons, deserts and lush rain forests, the highest mountains and deepest lakes. I flew into sprawling urban airports and tiny airstrips laid out in grasslands. I inhaled the exhaust fumes in city streets and the earthy smell after the rains came in the grasslands, decaying mangos, and the intoxicating fragrance of gardenia tree flowers. I tasted the sweet flavor of coconut and peanut sauces and that of bitter teas.

In *The Cobra's Heart,* the words of Ryszard Kapuściński beautifully express my feelings: "The continent is too large to describe. It is a veritable ocean, a separate planet, a varied, immensely rich cosmos. Only with the greatest simplification, for the sake of convenience, can we say 'Africa.' In reality, except as a geographical appellation, Africa does not exist."

Just imagine the differences encountered in the sixty-five countries I served. Governmental units were often formed in colonial times with no regard to the languages or people who lived in the areas. I had to learn ethnicity as opposed to nationality. Even though there were many similarities, to hold a meaningful conversation with leaders of African nations, I needed a great deal of information. I had to learn greetings, which were sometimes complicated. Kiss one cheek? Two cheeks? A greeting kiss on the lips? A proper greeting and visible respect were vitally important. Equally crucial was knowledge of political and ethnic backgrounds. It was a challenging role, yet these years form some of my fondest memories. I was exposed to new information in many ways, but I was eager to absorb and use it. It was a thrilling time. To me, there is no greater honor than to represent the United States on foreign soil.

I was happy to get to revisit Kenya. My friends there remembered me from the times I visited their homes and attended parties with them, but with the State Department, my role was more formal. I even had people along to protect me, and my interactions had to be very different. I did get to visit with my dear friend Christine Kenyatta, a graduate of Pennsylvania's Lehigh University and daughter of the late president of Kenya. She had put in place a curriculum in Kenya for the intellectually challenged.

I flew on Air Force Two (Air Force One becomes Air Force Two when the president is not on board) several times and faced a diplomatic quandary when hosting Maureen Reagan on the plane on a trip to Botswana and Mozambique. She was sensible and fun, but she was also President Reagan's daughter. I was in charge of that visit, and she wanted to meet privately to interview the president of Mozambique. This was not done. Standard operating protocol of the State Department requires that a note taker be present when talking to a foreign official. I knew I could lose my job if she was upset enough to report this incident negatively to her father. I struggled with the words to tell her no, sat her down, and explained the standard practices of diplomacy. Thankfully, she agreed to the American ambassador accompanying her and serving as the note taker.

Another stressful situation for me emerged in Equatorial Guinea. This is a quaint little country, the only Spanish-speaking country in Africa, bordered by Cameroon. My usual travel route to Equatorial Guinea was from a small airport in Cameroon on a tiny airplane. On this trip I had been charged with hand-delivering a personal letter from President Reagan to the president of Equatorial Guinea, Teodor Obiang Nguema Mbasogo. For most of the trip, I had carried it in my inside suit coat pocket, but for reasons I don't remember, I had slipped it in my bag.

When we landed on the runway, glistening and sticky with the heat of the tropics, I looked around for my bag, and it was nowhere to be seen. The ambassador greeted me with an entourage of officials and reminded me that the president was waiting. I explained that I must get my bag and felt myself getting warmer than my surroundings. The bag was simply gone, along with the rest of my career, I thought. We went on to meet President Mbasogo, and I tried to swallow my panic until the ambassador laughingly handed me my bag. "It happens all the time," he said. "Someone takes the wrong bag and returns it when the mistake is realized." The letter was found and delivered.

Back at home, I tried to simplify the very complex African world, to help Americans understand the issues in Ethiopia, our country's economic ties to the continent along with the private sector initiatives, the ancestral connection of thirteen million Americans due to enslavement of their ancestors in America, and the existence of the injustices and atrocities of South Africa.

The Ethiopian famine was a vivid illustration of our policies' importance to our objectives in Africa. A United States Agency for International Development (USAID) official dubbed it "Hell on Earth." A BBC reporter remembers parched countryside, bare hills, and weary and weakened men, women, and children congregated in places they thought they might find food. Mothers in worn embroidered calico dresses clutching emaciated children ran out into the road and risked their lives trying to stop vehicles and sell whatever possessions they still had, all to feed dying children. Thousands were dying every week. The famine killed one million people.

The United States was the largest single donor to the emergency relief there in 1985. We provided half of Africa's food shortfall in 1986. We were at the forefront in galvanizing contributions to one of the greatest tragedies of our time. We did this in a country whose government had been openly hostile to us. As the situation worsened and the emergency turned into a massive disaster, we told the Ethiopian government that we were prepared to provide massive assistance without regard to politics and the cool state of our relationship. We insisted that the aid be directly and thoroughly monitored. I believe this response spoke volumes to the Ethiopian people and, indeed, to all of Africa about our humanitarianism and our direct relevance to Africa's most pressing problems. People from every walk of life in Ethiopia thanked us. Our actions represented the best of America and the most telling response to the years of Soviet indifference. Soviet ideology and arms had dominated

Ethiopia, but the Soviet government failed to provide aid in terms of food. The shortage of food spread to other sub-Saharan countries, Sudan, Angola, and Cape Verde, and we continued to provide aid in these places. African governments were beginning to realize that they could no longer provide jobs for those citizens needing work and began looking to the private sector, not an instant panacea, but one that would make itself felt over several years.

Economically, there is a direct relationship between Africa's fortunes, its security, self-confidence, economic performance, political stability, and the growth of the Western world. Most African leaders recognized that the United States was committed to working with African nations on the basis of mutual interest. The challenge was to make our response relevant, to figuratively teach the African leaders how to fish rather than simply give them fish. The U.S. government led the world in providing emergency assistance, a value in food and money of one billion dollars in 1985, with additional contributions from private American organizations. These contributions were required in the face of drought, debt crisis, and political insecurity, but a careful, long-term development was necessary to maintain and expand self-sufficiency. This was not a foreign policy arena requiring government decisions but a personal incentive and market-based dialogue between potential private-sector business parties on two continents.

Restrictions imposed by bureaucracies have not worked long-term. The trend in the mid-1980s was a willingness of many African governments to divest themselves of government-operated industries and restrictions that had paralyzed economic evolution. They understood that private-sector growth correlated to economic expansion. Our appreciation of Africa's needs was solidified in President Reagan's statement of international investment policy in 1983, which recognized the vital contribution of foreign direct investment. Past investments were mostly by large multinationals like Goodyear, General Motors, Del Monte, Firestone, and Gillette, to name a few, rather than by smaller firms. Proposals during this period showed small businesses beginning to expand into Africa. Smaller businesses like flour mills and poultry and shrimp processing in Cameroon, wood treatment in Ghana, farm and seed production in Ivory Coast, a tractor plant in Kenya, fisheries in Nigeria, tannery and cosmetics in Botswana all seemed to better fit African needs. They were attentive to indigenous people, small by comparison, but relied on an additional layer of processing of existing resources and showed great chances of success. I made the case for potential small-business investment over and over, in open dialogues with African officials and private business-men and speaking before groups like the Trade and Investment Conference on Africa in Miami, the Sister Cities International Conference in Fort Worth, and anywhere else on either continent where people would listen to me. I tried to make the leaders of Africa understand that American companies did not have to go to Africa to make money and that for businesspeople to come, things had to be smooth. Airports had to be modernized and land transpor-tation needed to be seamless. The unwritten system of bribes couldn't stand the test of outside interests.

Working with the Department of Commerce, I arranged a two-day trade fair in Johannesburg in May 1986 that placed more than three hundred Americans and South Africans together to assess the assistance needed by Black South African business owners. At the fair, thirty-five South African businesses received manufacturing contracts for work from American busi-nesspeople. Fair participants underlined the need for an American presence in South Africa to help change racial policies in Johannesburg.

I dealt with many troubling, often horrendous, issues. Part of my job was to collect reports of human-rights violations from an American embassy official in each country and report back to Washington. Incidents included human trafficking, false arrests that were often political, imprisoning citizens without a trial or holding an unfair trial, and using the government to get rid of problems by killing their citizens.

22

GOALS IN AFRICA

In 1985, our basic goals in Africa included Namibian independence, Cuban troop withdrawal from Angola, withdrawal of Cuba and South Africa from Mozambique, a framework for regional security to end violence, and the elimination of apartheid in South Africa.

After my first trip to South Africa, my daughter, Victoria, called, bubbling with questions. "How was it?" she asked. "What did you see?"

I answered, "I can't tell you that. Call back in a few days." She may have thought I was too busy or there was too much to tell, but the truth was that I could not process and find words for what I had seen. In America, it was called segregation. In South Africa, it was called apartheid. In both places, it was racism. Watching Black South Africans brought memories of the systemic racism of my childhood back in nauseating waves. It angered me. It hurt me. It tried to break me and make me feel like I was second-class. I saw the people in South Africa who looked like me, and I could feel it all again. I could see the suffering in the way they walked, their eyes downcast, the lack of dreams, the anger at being stereotyped as unintelligent, lazy, and unimportant. Slavery, lynchings, and economic starvation had been their lot and ours. Many lives have been taken, and yet some of us lived in spite of it all. We refused to give up, give out, or give in.

Apartheid means "apart" in the Afrikaner language, and it was the slogan of the Afrikaner National Party. Their goal was to literally separate White people from those with a different color skin. The country was then run by Whites, who comprised only 12 percent of the population. Whether from superior force, fear, or hatred, the minority succeeded in terrorizing the majority from the 1940s to the 1990s.

People would then be treated differently based on their population group, the basis of apartheid. Offenses were dealt with using humiliation, cruelty, and often violence. Arrests, detention without trials, torture, assault, interrogations, beatings, shootings, and killings are all documented. Whites locked up or killed anyone who presented a problem. People suffered greatly.

The African National Congress (ANC), through its Programme of Action, encouraged strikes, mass actions, and civil disobedience. The logic was that the ruling class could not arrest everyone if large numbers of people defied and protested the unfair laws. A young lawyer named Nelson Mandela was part of this movement. In 1960, police attacked a demonstration. More than eighteen thousand were arrested, and sixty-nine were killed. The ANC was banned. In 1962, Nelson Mandela was arrested and sentenced to life in jail. The world finally reacted.

However, not everyone was against apartheid. Notable support came from the legacy of Cecil Rhodes, a British businessman made rich by the resources of Africa. His gifts founded Rhodes University and international study via the Rhodes Scholarship program. Rhodesia was named for him by his British South Africa Company.

Apartheid was entrenched by the time I was working in Africa. There were choices to be made by our government. President Reagan and the assistant secretary of state for African affairs pushed for expanded trade with Pretoria. I personally agreed and promoted the idea that economic and financial sanctions were not the way to go. We were criticized and accused of supporting apartheid, but we understood that sanctions were designed to break the country economically. We took steps to bring pressure on the system without attempting to destroy the economy and increase the suffering of the South African people. Concrete support for individuals and groups opposing apartheid was in place. Educational scholarships, institution building, unions, business development, human rights and legal defense funds were provided. We were planning the infrastructure for success beyond apartheid.

In my estimation, South Africa was going to move in one of two directions. Either Nelson Mandela and other ANC prisoners were going to be released and the Black majority (88 percent) with the White minority (12 percent) would get on with the task of forming a united government based on one man and one vote, or a civil war would ensue, so devastating that it would take years for the nation to recover, if ever. One of the surest ways to ignite a civil war was for Nelson Mandela to die in prison. He had to be freed without stipulations, or the country was doomed.

I wanted to see the release of Nelson Mandela and an economically strong South Africa with Black leadership. Continuing sanctions would have kept the future Black leaders from being successful. Why destroy the economy of South Africa and, indeed, the countries nearby? Sanctions would also impact the eight or nine surrounding countries that were dependent on the economy of South Africa. If South Africa went down the drain economically, so would these countries. The contributions and work of the majority population had built this strong economic structure. They, too, opposed apartheid but feared violence and economic retaliation if they voiced their opinion. This could come in the form of closed roads, workers being denied entry, power outages, and much more.

When Black governmental control came into being, the economy would weaken, and everyone would blame Black leadership. I believed and still think Africa needs the United States and the help we can provide through educational opportunities to ensure success in governing by Black leaders, unifying South Africa by creating a climate in which Blacks and Whites can work together in an equal partnership, and continuing the economic activities to strengthen their presence on the world market.

I also knew well the short memory of Americans and feared that if America decided to impose sanctions, Americans would feel that we had done our part and move on to something else. Even today, with all the problems remaining to face South Africa, there is little known in our country about South Africa's struggles. If American businesses honored sanctions and left, they may have never returned.

Each time I visited South Africa, I promoted the concept of economic strength to members of chambers of commerce, Jaycees, business entities, civic and government leaders as well as Black leaders. Destroying the economy was not the most important thing; rather, it was saving South Africa from itself. The White minority had committed such atrocities that it had put the country in this position. There were moments I felt ashamed as I told South Africans what to do. My own U.S. history offered a shameful example of the treatment of minorities. We had created terrible conditions: our government put Native Americans on reservations and upheld discriminatory laws by which Black people had to live. I love America, but it was hard to defend its wrongdoing, especially as I fought similar conditions in Africa.

In the 1970s, there was new hope as nearby Angola and Mozambique won independence from Portugal. Hope was cruelly dashed on June 16, 1976, when high school students led a demonstration protesting the Afrikaans Medium Decree of 1974. An estimated twenty thousand students filled the streets of Soweto, a Black township in Johannesburg, the name coming from the first two letters of each word in the name SOuth WEst TOwnship. Brutal police action followed, and officers fired on the students. Today, June 16 is a public holiday named Youth Day.

The South African government led by P. W. Botha was pushed into a state of emergency and began negotiating with Mandela. President Botha was a tough nut to crack. In 1989, Whites were still the minority and still controlled everything. The next South African president, F. W. de Klerk, engaged in secret discussions with Mandela, who was still in jail, then released him in 1990. In 1991, the de Klerk government began to repeal most of the legislation that provided the basis for apartheid. In 1994, the first democratic election was held from April 26 to 29. Millions stood in line to exercise their new right to vote, and voting lasted four days. April 27 has been celebrated as Freedom Day every year since. The new National Assembly's first act was to elect Nelson Mandela as president, the country's first Black chief executive and now "Father of his country." He saw national reconciliation as the main goal of his presidency. It was now the responsibility of the White minority to join Mandela and the Black majority to save South Africa. What was needed was a White minority leader to match the love and devotion for South Africa that Mandela showed.

Frederik Willem de Klerk sealed the deal. He and Mandela paved the way for a new South Africa. A strong economy was necessary for this to even be attempted. This event was the culmination and validation of my rationale, years before, and a strong reason to stay in the Reagan administration and work toward no economic sanctions for South Africa. Some say that President

Reagan didn't want sanctions in order to keep the country segregated. I hope this was not the case. It was certainly not what I wanted. President Reagan never asked me to quit anything I wanted to do. We had no arguments. I think that we enabled South Africa to survive, reorganize, and strengthen, and helped people there have more productive lives.

Apartheid laws had remained in effect for nearly fifty years. Many people suffered during this time, and many still suffer thirty years later. Often, the United States comes into a situation with good intentions, provides immediate help, and then leaves. South Africa needed our long-term help and still does.

As I traveled, speaking throughout our country, I challenged my audiences to learn as much about the world as possible, especially about Africa. They held the power to assist in the development of Africa. I suggested that they become better informed about Africa. Informed Americans eliminate misconceptions. Increased emphasis on the study of Africa from elementary school classrooms to university classes, families actually traveling to Africa, exchange programs such as Sister Cities, and inviting African exchange students to speak in our communities all help foster knowledge of the continent. I asked them to be aware of the array of African dance and music, for much cultural appreciation comes from the arts. We should not forget that there is a great deal to learn from the people of Africa.

During the years in Africa, I was honored by a number of individuals and organizations. One of the most memorable was when Coretta Scott King held my hand and said, "We appreciate you so much, Mr. Robertson." She led a delegation to South Africa to meet Winnie Mandela. I provided her information from the State Department. She felt that she and her group could make a change. She also visited when I was in Kenya. On that visit I offered her a Peace Corps volunteer placement "if she didn't have anything else to do." We all laughed.

Since I served as a presidential appointee, when President Reagan's term ended in January 1989, my role in Africa normally would have ended. I left the post a few months early to campaign for George H. W. Bush. At that time, I received a letter from Secretary of State George P. Shultz, who commended my service, writing: "During your extensive travels you have conveyed a message of hope, pride, and empathy on the vexing questions of southern Africa.

Using education as a vehicle of change was clearly reflected in your successful launching of a major new book program for disadvantaged South Africans." He was also pleased with my other endeavors such as the Sister Cities and shared my opinion of the importance of people-to-people programs. I valued his opinion of my work.

23

CONSULTING AND
MY FIRST LOVE

From 1988 to 1992, I worked for the Pagonis and Donnelly Group. This firm was a lobbying company with about twenty-five employees, the seventh-largest lobbying firm in the Washington, D.C., area at the time. I was a senior vice president and led the consulting part of the business, serving as a liaison between leaders of foreign governments and U.S. government and business leaders. Tom Donnelly was one of the founders of the group, and George Pagonis oversaw the merchandising side of the business. The group closed at the end of 1992.

I then formed my own consulting business, the Robertson Group. I represented American government leaders and international leaders. This job took me all over the world. One of my clients, General Bantubonke Harrington Holomisa, was from Transkei, the area where Nelson Mandela was born. Transkei was a nation created by South Africa, but it was not recognized by any country except South Africa. He supported the African National Congress and was quite an irritation to the South African government. Holomisa was like a son to Nelson Mandela, and working with him often included working with representatives of Mandela. I visited there many times. Neither I nor the United States could talk to the ANC, but I could gather information and provide advice to my client.

Apartheid was so truly wrong. In addition to my professional responsibilities to dismantle apartheid practices, I was resolved to personally do all I could to help the people affected. I used what I had. Through the Sister Cities program, we brought Black South African teachers to Camp Virginia Jaycee and provided teacher training, particularly for special-education teachers.

Another way to help was to provide educational materials to Black South African schools. Black schools in South Africa during apartheid were not funded properly; indeed, they were practically disregarded. When I visited, students learned to count in English in unison and by using bottle caps. There were no books. Many students came to school hungry and returned home, where no food was to be found. Yet, they valued education and felt it would produce a better quality of life for them. How could I return to the American land of plenty without helping?

Beginning with my time with the State Department and carrying over into the years of the Robertson Group, I worked with Dr. Barbara Ricks of the Center for Health, Education, and Economic Research (CHEER) to send millions of new books to disadvantaged populations around the world. Over one million books went to children who were victims of apartheid in South Africa. Dr. Ricks became a good friend. She owned a warehouse with access to surplus new books. We shipped texts for kindergarten through high school and college classes along with teacher editions, workbooks, practice books, tapes and duplicating masters, some with tapes and computer disks to accompany the educational programs. We provided ancillary materials to enhance the texts, and perhaps most important, preservice and in-service training for personnel who would be teaching using the materials.

I was able to go to the Hanover Primary School, housed in an old church building, near Bhisho in South Africa in 1994 to present the first shipment to the East Cape. The principal told students that Hanover School was chosen as the first school to receive textbooks because it was a symbol of the community's determination to keep a school going under adverse circumstances. The children were awed by the solemnity of the occasion but broke out into song to welcome me. The school officials and students expressed so much gratitude for the books. I asked the boys and girls "to promise to learn, grow, dream and do their best to ensure they, as leaders of the new South Africa, gave what was necessary." By 1995, we had shipped six million books to sixty-two countries, the majority of which were distributed in Africa. According to Dr. Ricks, CHEER shipped approximately eighteen million books valued at approximately $1 billion to seventy-eight countries, or 43 percent of the countries in the world, during the 1990s.

I was a board member of Books for the World and also helped get funding from the Bureau of Indian Affairs to provide books for children on Indian reservations. I solicited funds from a variety of sources to provide books to children and families in developing countries.

At the same time, I continued to speak all over the United States, from university graduations to prayer breakfasts, with the goal of bringing people of the world together.

President George H. W. Bush appointed me to the Take Pride in America Committee, a twenty-one-member group established by the Department of the Interior. Our goal was to promote and celebrate national stewardship and creation of public lands by individuals, civic groups, and corporations. Awareness of volunteer opportunities and annual awards for activism in protecting public spaces were promoted by the committee. Linda Evans, star of the television show *Dynasty,* once posed with us for a publicity photo. One of my duties in this assignment was to sell the idea of clean riverbeds. I spoke at colleges and civic groups to push for this specific care of the environment. I was also the cochair of the Federal Task Force on Disabilities.

Personally, this was a turbulent time for me. Johnnie and I had grown apart. After forty years of marriage, we separated. Our children were grown and gone. I was working out of a nice office in my home, but I missed getting dressed and going in to work.

In 1999, I lost two siblings: my older sister, Faye, sixty-six, and my younger brother Jackie Frank Louis, fifty-two. Faye had settled in Pittsburgh and worked in food services and raised a daughter, Wadine Henrietta. Jackie had married a girl from Mississippi, Zelmer Batemon, and moved there. Jackie had been an outstanding athlete, playing both football and basketball in high school in Roanoke, and served in the U.S. Army.

A class reunion at Lucy Addison High School was planned for the summer of 1992, and I decided to return to Roanoke and visit my former home. There I reconnected with my childhood friend and high school sweetheart, Ruth Price Beard. I had fallen in love with her at age sixteen. I got the chance to dance with her, held her closely, and discovered that I wasn't falling in love with her . . . but that I had never fallen out of love with her. When I left

Roanoke to go to Bluefield State, she had gone to school in Baltimore. During my freshman year, I had asked her to wait and marry me when I graduated, and she had said no, disrupting my life's plan.

Now, forty-some years later, she was divorced, had two grown daughters, and had returned from working overseas as an Internal Revenue Service auditor. She'd gone halfway around the world, and I'd gone halfway around the world, and all of a sudden here was my sweetheart from high school.

We managed a long-distance relationship between her home in Florida and mine in Northern Virginia for several years and married on February 1, 2000, in Washington, D.C. I dearly love her. She was a golfer but has traded golf for bridge and is currently a competitive bridge player, participating in national tournaments. Our life together is comfortable; after all, we've known each other since eighth grade. We began dating in our junior year, attending ball games and dances and parties together. Our senior prom portrait taken fifty years earlier, showing us with our hands entwined, is now displayed in our home.

24

BACK TO SCHOOL

After we married, Ruth became instrumental in my work, sharing ideas, writing, organizing, and philanthropy. I moved to Florida to be with Ruth in her home. It was strange to sit out on the deck in the sunshine on Christmas Day, but she loved Florida, and I loved her. Our lives were full. We enjoyed the theater, music, sports, and got on the dance floor as often as we could.

I was active in raising money for Camp Virginia Jaycee and traveled to speak at fund-raisers for my alma mater, Bluefield State College. But it wasn't enough.

Somehow, I felt in the way. She had her friends and her daily schedule, and I didn't. I was getting up early and getting dressed in a suit and tie to go to Barnes & Noble or Borders Books to read and study. I was driving my wife crazy. I needed to get up in the morning and go to work. I needed a reason to get out of bed.

I'd had all these experiences. Why not share them, especially with children? If I could change one child, it would change both our lives.

It was clear that I needed a job, so I attended a job fair for teachers. I was interviewed and my credentials were praised, but I was sixty-nine years old. The first day of the fair, I struck out. I was told that I'd be wonderful at an inner-city school; Sligh Middle School was mentioned. The principal wasn't there, but she arrived on the second day of the fair and interviewed me. She asked what my long-term goal was, and I told her, "to teach at Sligh Middle School." Then she asked what my short-term goal was, and I told her, "to teach at Sligh Middle School."

There were concerns. Could I relate to the children? Were the children too young to have me as a teacher? Could I manage a rowdy classroom? Once again, there was a divine presence watching out for me, this time in the form of that middle school principal, Ms. Juanita Underwood. She took a chance and offered me a job as a language arts teacher. She gave me the opportunity I wanted and allowed me to share firsthand the experience of my lifetime with young teenagers.

I was watched carefully in my language arts classroom the first few days, but I must have quieted the concerns because I taught there for the next ten years. Ms. Underwood became my biggest supporter. A teaching position in American history opened up a year or so later, and the door of opportunity was further cracked ajar. I was going to teach about the country I love.

In 1970, some thirty-two years earlier, I had given a speech about education at the Jaycees Outstanding Young Educator dinner honoring Edward E. Rhea of Allegheny High School in Virginia. I spoke the beliefs of my heart: "These young people are the greatest resource we have—they are the key to the future and it is up to us as educators to mold them to become good citizens of their community, state, and nation. How do we teach them? In the 1970s, do we still use the textbook as the classroom 'Bible' and the only educational tool? Do we teach students only as a group rather than as individuals? If this is the type of teaching we are doing, our state's future is in jeopardy."

I had a second chance to implement my lofty expectations of educators. I used all the media I could find to take students down my memory lane, the history of our country as it was made in the twentieth century. I used newspaper clippings, photographs, even works of literature. It was said that my life was an "American Journey," which was also the name of our textbook. My classroom was sparsely decorated, the way I wanted it, with the Bill of Rights, the U.S. Constitution, and cameos of the presidents on the walls. All great educators must have a little bit of entertainer in them, and I tried to make my classroom interactive and thought-provoking. I dressed as Abraham Lincoln and delivered the Gettysburg Address to a group of teachers and students. Shortly after entering the classroom, I had students repeat in unison the thought for the day. Here is an example from Thomas Paine: "Those who expect to reap the blessings of freedom must . . . undergo the fatigue of supporting it." We'd state the classroom rules aloud: "Be respectful! Be responsible! Be safe! Be a learner!" Then, I'd ask, "What is it we are here to do today?" and they would answer, "Prepare to become president." This was before Barack Obama was elected president. They didn't think they could be president, but I told them that they could.

I had an urgent set of mantras: "You've got to succeed. You can't falter. You've got to repay; you've got to give back." I wanted them to know that this was what life is all about.

One of my colleagues, Tywanna Henderson, twenty-eight at the time, an English teacher in the classroom next door, was very kind to me. "He holds our team together," she said. "I've never heard him say anything negative, even when the kids are 'very animated,' as he says. He says if you harp on the negative, that's the way you're going to feel. His outlook is just inspiring."

I believed that it was hard for youngsters to be what they cannot see, and so even my presence at the school was valuable in creating positive mind-sets among the students. I dressed in a suit and tie. Some years I had perfect attendance. I did my best to model the values I taught: hard work, motivation, citizenship, responsibility, and the dignity of service to others. If a picture is worth a thousand words, think what a living role model in daily life is worth.

I collaborated with the Tampa Chapter of the Links, Inc., and coordinated the African-American Read-In at Sligh Middle School from 2007 to 2011. This annual event was part of a statewide effort to encourage literacy and pride in literature of diverse origins whereby schools, community groups, churches, book clubs, and families are invited to come together during the month of February to read African American–inspired literature. We all read some powerful books, learning about other lives, even worlds, to model and experience the joy of reading together.

In the 2005–6 school term, I was the oldest teacher in the system and was nominated for Teacher of the Year. I earned a place as one of the top ten finalists in a district of nearly fifteen thousand teachers.

I had left the classroom in 1970 to go to work for Governor Holton. In 2002 I went back. The child in my classroom had changed. This new child had more freedom, he or she demanded more freedom and was more independent. Their lives at home were very different, and in many ways they were raising themselves. These children had more chemicals in their lives in terms of drugs. They had less respect for the teacher.

However, there were commonalities. Athletics still met the needs of many children. I had coached before, and I coached again. These students were still as curious as those from thirty years before. I tried to expose them to things they hadn't seen before. Many had never left the state, and I started thinking about ways to bring them to Virginia.

I watched my students in the summertime and knew that they stayed in neighborhoods where drugs were sold. Two organizations in the school, "Men of Vision," which served at-risk boys and strived to teach them to grow up to be responsible men, and "GEMS" (Girls Empowered by Mentorship), seemed like logical places to start. I created a summer trip to expose the students to another environment. We flew from Florida to Virginia and took the students to Camp Virginia Jaycee, where they assisted counselors with special-needs campers. They set up crafts classes, helped with swimming, and did a variety of jobs supervised by the counselors. With 94 percent of Sligh Middle School students qualifying for free or reduced lunches, for many of these youngsters this was their first flight and the first time they had ever seen mountains. During the trip, we toured Bluefield State College. They saw where I had been educated and got a taste of college life. They visited the archives where my documents and awards were displayed.

When it was time to go home to Tampa, they had gained so much they did not want to leave. They were beginning to understand and believe that their lives really did matter. They were serving others, the disabled, and they felt good about themselves. They had learned that people with disabilities were wonderful people who wanted the same things they did. Their horizons had expanded.

"I look forward to their trip each year," an official with the college remarked. "They remind me why I chose to be a fund-raiser in higher education. The young men dress in white shirts and ties, speak respectfully, and display genuine enthusiasm for learning. They give me hope for the future and renew my commitment to make education possible for such students."

When the program began, I personally raised from five thousand to seven thousand dollars each year to make these trips happen, but later we needed financial assistance to continue the program.

In 2014, Dr. Angela Vickers, the Sligh Middle School principal, accompanied us. "I felt like a parent, not a principal," she said. Three of the student participants spoke about their experience.

Pierre Alsint, a rising high school freshman, called the time "a life-changing experience." In his journal he defined a real man as "a male who has his priorities right. He helps people in need, and although he will make mistakes, he builds off that experience and perseveres." Alsint wanted to be a doctor or a lawyer or play in the NFL. He loved sports but believed that academics and hard work must come before sports.

Another rising freshman, Ty'rek English, eyed a future in law or sports medicine. "I don't look at a person with disabilities; I look at them as a person," he said. He wrote that a "real man is brave and powerful and a leader and cares for his family and loves his wife and kids."

Devin Johnson, a rising eighth-grader, called the experience an awakening. "No matter how hard you think your life is, somebody's life is harder," he said. To him a real man admits his mistakes and takes care of his children. He was drawn in the direction of sports medicine as a future calling.

Another student who participated in the program, James Elissant, went on to attend Tampa Bay Tech, and was the first of my Sligh students to work summers at Camp Virginia Jaycee while he attended college.

I preached consistently that, with a sense of responsibility and hard work, my students could succeed. Over an eight-year period more than eighty young men and women participated. As far as I know, we have not lost even one of those students to the system, that is, none have entered the criminal justice system and gone to prison. Our school system was very supportive of my efforts.

Out of this successful program, I had an idea for the future: to bring inner-city children from all over the country as eighth-graders to Bluefield State College for summer camp. Expose them to the possibility of a college education. Stay in touch with these teenagers, and some would see the need to continue their lives as college students at Bluefield State College or elsewhere.

I taught until I was seventy-nine years old. Justin George, reporter for the *Tampa Bay Times*, wrote: "It was an odd picture: 79-year-old William B. Robertson, a history teacher who wears cufflinks and has served five U.S. presidents, mingling with kids wearing braces and struggling to push past adolescence. He will leave behind a legacy that school officials say surpasses Sligh's walls—let alone Tampa's city limits."

I tried to explain how college was within their reach. Those kids can go much further than I could go; they can go much further than I ever even dreamed of going. That's the reason I taught. These children did not grow up in a segregated society, relegated to schools and limited to certain stores, restaurants, and even jobs based on the color of their skin. Their schools were not considered inferior; their teachers were not considered inferior. They have lived during a time when a Black man served this great country as president of the United States. As I stood on the shoulders of those who came before, so these children have had their way made easier. Many obstacles, both in public attitude and policy, have been removed from their paths. Make no mistake, hurdles remain for us all, but the way is much better lighted for them than it was for my father and for me. However, these students must have the assurance that America feels that Black lives matter, not that they are still considered second-class citizens.

I had come full circle from my first love and profession. I loved every one of my students, and they seemed to like my way of explaining history. I think most understood the subject matter, and I hope that, with better understanding of our great country, they felt optimistic. Each class, every day, each child in the classroom has something unique that can lead to his or her success. As a teacher, I just had to find it. I enjoyed teaching tremendously, and I like to think it was mutually beneficial. To this day, I am in touch with many of my former students and colleagues and get invitations to breakfast, to lunch, and to visit. We host a picnic in the summer for current and former students. They begin calling in the spring to remind me to set a date. They enjoy bringing me up-to-date on their accomplishments, and I enjoy hearing about them. I hope I have enriched their lives. They certainly have enriched mine.

25

MY FAMILY

Separate from my work, but often on my mind through the years, were members of my large family, my siblings, their children, and, of course, my daughter and son. My brothers had spread throughout the country; most of them had joined a branch of the military and were led by their military assignments, employment opportunities, and, for those who married, the hometowns of their wives.

In 2007, my youngest brother, Vincent Courtney, passed away at age fifty-four. Another brother and I had nicknamed him "Buster" at birth. He had been a sixteen-pound baby. His birth was difficult, and it affected his left arm. As a child, he spent months in the Shriners Hospitals getting help with his bad arm, but he excelled in athletics in spite of his disability. Buster graduated from Lucy Addison High School and earned an associate degree from National Business College in Roanoke. He lived in Wilmington, Delaware, where he worked for Amtrak and raised three sons, Cory, Clifford, and Stokely.

James Hucksey Barry, my brother six years my junior, died in 2016 at age seventy-seven. He was in the Lucy Addison marching band in high school and then spent twenty years in the U.S. Navy. He lived in Jacksonville, Florida, and had five children and several grandchildren, all dear to me. They live in the Roanoke area.

In 2017, I lost my last surviving brother, Patrick Gardner Robertson, who passed away at age seventy-seven. He had a rich singing voice and had been a regular performer in the early 1950s on the Saturday-morning teen programs at WSLS television station in Roanoke. He graduated from Lucy Addison and sang in the school choir. Patrick served honorably in the U.S. Army during the Vietnam era. He traveled extensively throughout Europe and the United States. When he returned to Roanoke, singing became his passion, and many Sunday mornings he could be found serving as guest soloist at various churches. Also, he developed a fondness for comedy and delighted many in Roanoke with comedy and songs at the Roanoke Comedy Club. Failing health confined Patrick to the Virginia Veterans Care Center for the last quarter century of his life. Yet, his voice was rarely silent. He was called upon to render patriotic songs at the facility on holidays such as the Fourth of July and Veterans Day. His tombstone at the Southwest Virginia Veterans Cemetery in Dublin, Virginia, reads, "God Needed a Baritone."

My last living sibling, Ellen Marie, resides in Roanoke in a nursing home. She was by far the best athlete in the family, born before the time when she would have won scholarships for her prowess. Marie graduated from a girls' school, St. Francis de Sales in Powhatan, Virginia, and went on to finish at Siena Heights College, a Catholic girls' school in Ohio. She studied to become a Catholic nun and spent her life in social work, a great deal of it in inner cities.

Most cherished by me, of course, are my children, Bernice Victoria and William Allen.

Recently, they both reflected on their childhood. Victoria remembers: "I feel that I grew up as a normal child who was brought up in a special way. I attended Gilmer Elementary School while [my father] taught there. I remember preparing for the first day of school. I am left-handed and my father told me if a teacher tries to change my hand, they were to 'come see him.' We were a team! However, I learned very quickly because he was the only male teacher at Gilmer, he was father, disciplinarian, mentor, leader, and support to all the children. I had to be an example for the other children and I had to share him with them as well. I didn't mind much because wherever I went, whatever I did, I was referred to as 'Mr. Robertson's daughter.' I was protected from bullies and given the benefit of the doubt from my teachers when I got into trouble or forgot my homework, just a few perks to compensate for my efforts!

"We lived in our own African American community. Our schools were regulated by segregation. As a result, we all knew one another or knew of one another in Roanoke. I attended the same junior high and high school that my father and his family attended. There was great comfort and pride in our circle of friends and community. I even had teachers who taught my father and were still teaching when I came of age. I was expected to do well, and I did.

"By 8th or 9th grade, my father founded a summer camp for those individuals who are differently abled, Camp Virginia Jaycee, through the Jaycee organization. My classmates called me 'Apple Jelly' because the Jaycees statewide decided to sell apple jelly to raise funds to buy the land for the camp. My classmates read about that in the newspaper. I didn't mind this teasing; my classmates weren't aware of how great this mission was. My brother and I were not allowed to work at the camp because my father didn't want people to think he created the camp in order to employ his children. So, I worked in another capacity. I raised funds for the camp from friends, work associates, neighbors, and companies. Camp Virginia Jaycee was a member of the Robertson family, and now we are recipients of its legacy."

Victoria graduated from John Marshall High School in Richmond in 1973 and enjoyed cheerleading there. Then she attended Virginia Tech, decided that dancing was her calling, and graduated from the Alvin Ailey School of Dance in New York. She became a model and dancer in Virginia, New York, and in Nairobi, Kenya. She starred in productions such as *The Merry Widow, Jesus Christ, Superstar,* and *Kiss Me, Kate.* She also participated in a Disney Thanksgiving Day parade. Victoria provided valuable assistance as I worked with Peace Corps volunteers in Kenya and Seychelles. She visited Denmark, Italy, Ghana, Liberia, Kenya, and Seychelles on the job with me. Later in life, she became a meditation instructor. She describes her experience: "In 1993, I started to study Vipassana meditation. Vipassana means insight, to see things as they really are, one of India's most ancient techniques of meditation, worldwide. I took my first courses in Shelburne Falls, Massachusetts, a ten-day residency. We learned to meditate for nine and a half hours a day. Once I took this silent retreat and experienced the benefits, I was motivated to share the experience with others. I traveled to India several times to continue my study of this technique and was eventually appointed an assistant teacher. Both my parents have taken a Vipassana course. Interestingly, I met a few Vipassana meditators who lived on Bent Mountain, Virginia, not very far from Camp Virginia Jaycee, and we decided, with my father's permission and S. N. Goenka's blessings, to create off-center Vipassana courses at Camp Jaycee. We held ten-day residential silent retreats twice yearly during the camp's off-season for eleven years. The rent for the courses went directly to the camp, and meditation was shared for the benefit of many in Southwest Virginia. Again, my father and me, a team!"

Currently, Victoria lives and works in New York City.

Allen attended Henrico High School and Blacksburg High School and graduated from Herndon High School, all three schools in Virginia, then attended Virginia Commonwealth University. He played varsity basketball at each school and was a member of the jazz and marching bands at all three schools as well as a member of the Roanoke Youth Symphony Orchestra. He was a member of the Nairobi Symphony Orchestra and played bassoon for the National Theater in Nairobi. Allen was appointed to a cultural position, board member of ArtSpace Herndon, by the mayor of Herndon. He has mastered a variety of musical instruments, including seven woodwinds. In addition to teaching guitar, Allen plays and sings professionally in the style of Nat King Cole. He also produces music and puts together musical groups. "Music dominates my life," he admits. Allen remembers knowing early on that he was the son of an (in his words) incredible person. "As a youngster, I honestly wished that I could have had more time with him for myself. We had to share him with so many others."

He married Cynthia Powell from Stoystown, Pennsylvania, in August 1992, and they have two children, Eva Marie, who lives and works in Northern Virginia, and Teddy Allen, who also graduated from Herndon High and is currently attending Northern Virginia Community College.

26

THE SAD DEMISE OF CAMP VIRGINIA JAYCEE

During this period, I was delivering a great many speeches, but all honoraria went to Camp Virginia Jaycee, my favorite charity. The Virginia Jaycees saw the camp as their premier project. For almost fifty years, they did maintenance through work parties, funded many "camperships," and protected the facility in every manner possible.

When membership in the Jaycees declined significantly, it was felt that the camp needed to be protected in case of bankruptcy or anything negative that would take place with the Jaycee organization. Therefore, for the sum of $100,000, the camp was put in the hands of a holding group, Dare to Care, which had several former high-ranking Virginia Jaycees on the governing body. A new group was formed at Camp Virginia Jaycee to carry out the camping program. The two entities did not function well together, and Dare to Care did not maintain the property as agreed. I requested the late attorney William B. Poff to bring the parties together to get things back on track, but he could never get Dare to Care to come to the negotiating table.

Dare to Care gave the property to HopeTree Family Services, an affiliate of the Baptist General Association of Virginia, in 2012 without any consultation with the Virginia Jaycees or Camp Virginia Jaycee. Upon hearing the news of the facility going to HopeTree, Tom King, board chairman of Camp

Virginia Jaycee, and I contacted HopeTree and told them that we would like to have our facility back.

We were basically told we could retrieve it for what HopeTree had put in it financially. This is what we requested: that Camp Virginia Jaycee, the facility the Virginia Jaycees founded, maintained, and operated, which served more than forty-seven thousand children and adults with intellectual and developmental disabilities, be returned to its rightful owners, and that it be returned to the Virginia Jaycees for the sum of a firm $450,000, offered by a good Samaritan.

HopeTree had held the title to the camp for five years, which, they reported, were money-losing years. They planned to auction it in December 2017 at a minimum price of $600,000. That auction didn't happen and was rescheduled for March. Again, the auction was delayed. In May, the auction took place, but no bidder offered the minimum price.

When I heard HopeTree officials say no maintenance was done at the camp since it opened in 1971 until they came along, it was a slap in the face to the Jaycees. Fundraising and maintenance were everyday efforts. Jaycee chapters adopted cabins, thus providing furniture for them, new roofing was installed when needed, and toilets and sinks were repaired and replaced. I believed HopeTree tried to gain too much credit and inflated the amount they spent.

Over the years the camp helped both special-needs people and their parents. It allowed parents to plan vacations. The camp also offered respite camps on weekends that gave parents a chance to rest. In 2002, I went to Tampa, Florida, to live after having raised between $600,000 and $700,000 between 1998 and 2002 for Camp Virginia Jaycee. This money was to have been spent for camperships and maintenance. I am not aware of Dare to Care or HopeTree accounting for these funds.

I began teaching middle school in Tampa and found special-needs students of a different kind. I had students whose environments were filled with drive-by shootings and drugs. I made arrangements with Camp Virginia Jaycee officials to bring ten to twelve well-chaperoned seventh-graders from my school and several others to serve as junior counselors. They cleaned tables and floors, helped to feed physically disabled campers, kept equipment in order, worked at the pool, and acted as supervised "junior" counselors. These inner-city student volunteers have been honored by Presidents Obama and Trump.

Special-education teachers from Kenya, Black townships in South Africa, and Sierra Leone had visited the camp and been trained in camp administration for the disabled. They returned to their countries and started similar facilities.

Management of the camp should have never gotten to this point. We, the Virginia Jaycees, should have provided better oversight. Before accepting the offer of free land, HopeTree should have consulted the Virginia Jaycees and the Camp Virginia Jaycee board. Nothing is really free!

If the facility had been returned, everyone would have been a winner, especially those with special needs, because we would have kept alive the joy, love, and hope this unique ninety-acre facility, Camp Virginia Jaycee, has put forth to help change the world.

A letter from Christie Thomas, a longtime volunteer worker at Camp Virginia Jaycee, summarized the feelings of many: "I looked into a pair of sad eyes this summer [2018], soulful eyes, as our camper said, 'Camp Jaycee is home. I want to go home.'

"All I could say was, 'I know,' because I do know. What's happened to camp isn't right and it isn't fair. Camp Jaycee is Bill Robertson's legacy. He had a vision for camp during a time when 'mentally retarded' was an acceptable term for our population. He knew our campers needed a safe space to recreate long before 'safe space' became a catchword.

"Times have changed, vocabulary has changed, and standards have changed, but the thing that never changed about Camp Jaycee is that it always remained a traditional outdoor camping experience. In its nearly 50 years, Camp Jaycee never significantly changed its program, never became steeped in technology or anything fancy. It has always been about the old-school, traditional camping experience: campfires, fishing, swimming, mosquito bites.

"Our campers want to come back. Our staff wants to come back and introduce a new generation to the relentless humidity of a Virginia summer, to the red clay of Roanoke that never really comes out of clothes, to campfires, s'mores, and mosquito bites."

I revisited it just before the sale, and tears came to my eyes when I saw the weeds and the broken fences. Surveying the scene, my mind played tricks on me. I thought I could hear the splashing of children learning to swim, the shrieks of joyful children's laughter. I remembered the counselors, exhausted but smiling at the end of the day. In my mind, I saw women from Africa teaching American youngsters about gardening and watched inner-city youth as they realized how they could help others. I felt the passion that had created this space and the love it spread to those most in need. I mentally watched a video fast-forward of a little girl in a wheelchair who had attended the camp every single year and grew into a middle-aged woman with white hair. I smiled at the remembered foolishness of teenage counselors entertaining and hosting parties for the campers. How could I let it go? I fought on.

A last-ditch effort to encourage HopeTree to accept the $450,000 came in the form of an online Save Camp Virginia Jaycee petition. More than 1,800 signatures were on the document, but the HopeTree board of directors did not respond to requests to meet. I repeatedly requested them to come to the negotiating table to iron out differences and give us a chance to regain the camp, but to no avail.

HopeTree sold the facility to a Christian rescue operation, Crisis Response International, for $610,000 in March 2019. In the deal, HopeTree was able to maintain 3.5 acres and a group home on the property for its own use. The group made a substantial profit off the work of thousands of people of goodwill, including the Jaycees and local supporters and volunteers. I had personally spent countless thousands of dollars. I even had taken out a life insurance policy in honor of my Roanoke and Tampa students, payable to Camp Virginia Jaycee, to provide camperships after my death.

After forty-eight years, the camp launched by the Virginia Jaycees for special-needs children and adults, my life's work, no longer existed.

The demise of Camp Virginia Jaycee was the lowest point in my life; however, I blame no one but myself. Even though I was holding down a full-time job and serving as the number-one fund-raiser and cheerleader for the camp, I should have been more involved in hands-on management decisions.

27

RENAISSANCE AT BLUEFIELD STATE COLLEGE

While I was grieving the loss of Camp Virginia Jaycee and the future needs of disadvantaged individuals that I believed would be unmet, there was a change coming, unknown to me. God intervened in my life once again. It was as if He spoke, saying, "No, no, no, you didn't fail," and picked me up with the event just around the corner, a golden thread in my life that sparkled brightly.

I had been asked to speak at graduation at Bluefield State College in the spring of 2019. I prepared as I had for hundreds of speeches before, but this one was with a heavy heart. My motivation was lacking. I thought perhaps I was tired and felt sure that I was exhibiting signs of depression. I reminded myself how important Bluefield State College was to me. As I wrote, I felt better, and I was able to end the speech with directives from the bottom of my heart to provide housing for students, to advocate for the college and for the City of Bluefield, to provide services and activities for students to provide vigor to the campus, and to hire people of color. The celebration of the fifty-year anniversary of the graduation of the Class of 1969 was a happy reminder that Bluefield State was here to stay.

My speech ended to applause and the awarding of diplomas. I expected to exit with the speakers and the faculty. Moments later, the school's president, Robin Capehart, announced: "The Bluefield State College Board of

Governors, by unanimous vote, has chosen to honor Mr. Robertson in the rededication of our school's library in his name, the William B. Robertson Library." He explained further that a proclamation signed by BSC board chair Garry Moore saluted my "career in education and public service in which he would pass along to others the gift of wisdom and inspiration he had received" at Bluefield State.

This was a surprise to me. I had donated month by month to the library over the years but not with this honor in mind. The library was previously named for Wendell Hardway, the school's president during the 1970s. He presided over unrest, the closing of the dorms, and protest bombings along with the replacement of Black professionals with White colleagues from his former college, upsetting the alumni of our traditionally Black college. My name on the library was said to be a fresh beginning, a renaissance for the institution.

28

CALL TO ACTION

My life has been quite a journey. I was a Bobby Kennedy Democrat. I served Linwood Holton, the finest governor Virginia, or any other state, has ever had. I was fortunate to have become acquainted with President George H. W. Bush and Barbara Bush and to serve them. I stand strongly in the Barack and Michelle Obama arena, and I campaigned for President Obama during both election campaigns in Florida. That's who I am.

I didn't always agree with the policies of every president I served, but within the framework of what they wanted me to do, I was also able to do the things I wanted to do. I was allowed to assist those who were locked outside of the mainstream. In other words, I had my own program in addition to theirs.

I realized that every president I served had good qualities in spite of any difference of opinion the two of us may have had. These individuals, like many others, taught me the value of being dedicated to a cause.

I have been asked more than once if I didn't get angry about political chicanery and obvious injustice. Yes, I was outraged many times, but I only allowed it to flame inside me. Over the years I learned to set my thermostat to "calm restraint" on the outside. Furious reactions seldom create lasting change; peaceful communication always has a better chance. My goal was to initiate effective, long-term change. I had learned as a Little League coach that anger did not lead to victory. As I mentioned before, I always want to win. To be the voice for others, especially for those unable or untrained to speak for themselves—minorities, those in poverty, the disabled, and at-risk youth—is a fight worth fighting. The prize, fair opportunities for those denied them, is worth the self-control. That's who I am, as well.

The only regret I have is not doing more to help America realize the true dreams of inalienable life, liberty, and happiness for all citizens. The United States, this great country in which we live, was not built by any one group. America is a great nation, but until we recognize that hands of many colors made it what it is, we will not progress. We pledge "liberty and justice for all" in classrooms daily, but not everyone believes in this concept. Until that phrase becomes reality, we fool ourselves to think we can achieve greatness without equality for all. Our diversity is our strength. One group is not superior to another. Equal opportunity makes us stronger.

Nelson Mandela expressed my life's calling when he said: "I have cherished the ideal of a democratic and free society in which all persons live together in harmony with equal opportunities. It is an ideal which I hope to live for and to achieve." The sparkling thread of equal opportunity runs across the tapestry of my life and has grown brighter in places, but, sadly, some stitches are yet to be sewn. I must point out those gaps and the underlying fabric ranging from our history of slavery and segregation, to the conversations Black parents must have with their sons, to the future of my college alma mater, Bluefield State College, and finally, to current conditions regarding "squeegee boys," the pandemic, and the courage of a young football player.

All of us did not come here of our own accord. Many of us can trace our heritage to Africa, where our ancestors were kidnapped, placed in the holds of ships carrying enslaved people in filth and subhuman conditions, and brought to this country. We were not immigrants but rather objects, nonhumans, free labor. We were enslaved by people who were seeking freedom and a better life for themselves, their children and grandchildren. They spoke of all men being created equal and the promise of life, liberty, and the pursuit of happiness, but they did not provide or permit the same for the captives.

In 1861, the Civil War began. There are those who say the war was a stand for states' rights and the right to own slaves. The land of the free and the home of the brave became a haven for slavery and the total domination of a race of human beings. The Civil War cannot be romanticized. Utilizing the whip on naked backs in the hot sun of America's South and other parts of the country only benefited the "owners" of the enslaved people who built this nation free of charge and against their will. One man owning another is always, in every way, wrong.

In many ways we continue this war. Even today, we are looked upon as unintelligent people who need to be kept in their place, wherever that is. Menial jobs and substandard housing have been reserved for us. The criminal justice system is not our friend; it works against us. People fear us, knowing little or nothing about us. School textbooks identify Booker T. Washington and George Washington Carver as the only true heroes we have produced. We have been stereotyped and looked upon with disdain, Yet, we have shed blood and given our lives in every war America has fought. People say that it is Donald J. Trump, president of the United States, who promotes this type of thinking. No, he is divisive, but this thinking has been there since the first Blacks were brought to these shores four hundred years ago.

My daughter is now in her sixties, but she remembers wanting to go to Lakeside Amusement Park in Salem, Virginia, when she was eight years old. She was not able to enjoy the activities there because of the color of her skin, and her father could do nothing about it. She thought it was something she did. She was raised in a middle-class family and has traveled to Europe and Africa, but she remembers Lakeside, her first brush with racism. Just think of the number of Black citizens whose minds are affected by something they couldn't control, the evil of racism.

Poor schools were thought to be adequate for us. At the time just before the Supreme Court, in *Brown v. Board of Education*, rejected the nation's separate-but-equal policy for public schools, Black students from Giles County, Virginia, were rising at 4:00 a.m. to ride a bus to Park Central High in Bluefield, West Virginia. They had to leave after classes for their home, in another state, at 3:00 p.m., deprived of sports and clubs.

I grew up in segregated Roanoke, and I knew most of its neighborhoods from selling newspapers, but I felt cut off from the totality of life in the city. We lived in segregated communities in tiny decrepit houses right on top of each other. I try to control any feeling of anger over years of segregation because I can't dwell on it. You have to get on with your business. I learned in coaching that if you get mad, you don't win, and I always want to win.

At my school, Lucy Addison High, we got the things Jefferson High threw away, like old books and old football equipment. The Black schools were clearly treated as second-class facilities. I was sustained by the kinship, the bond, and the extended family of Roanoke's Black community, by home, school, and church. I can still name every teacher in the 1940s who urged me to strive and excel because a better day was coming. I didn't have a White teacher until graduate school at Radford University.

As a Black father, I try to teach my children not to allow themselves to get hurt, to work toward not always having their defenses up. White fathers do not have to have the same conversation. They and their sons have a sense of freedom in America that it is lacking for those of us who are Black. In essence, they and the system are one. Very few Black males escape experiencing a situation where a White authority figure, often a police officer, treats them differently because of the color of their skin. I thought that I had made that escape, but five years ago, at age eighty-two, living in Tampa, Florida, I was pulled over by the police.

It was a Sunday morning and I had just left Mass at my church, St. Peter Claver Church. I was dressed in a suit and tie, driving a Buick Le Sabre, a car that many young people call "an old man's car." I was driving north on Nebraska Avenue and made a left turn heading east to get to the interstate. As I made the turn, I noticed flashing lights in my rearview mirror and a police car moving up fast behind me.

I knew everything was in order. I had all of my papers. I was not speeding, and I had signaled properly to turn. I moved to the side and stopped. A plain-clothes officer jumped out of the passenger side of the police car. He came up to my car quickly and bellowed, "Whose car is this?" He did not say "Good morning, sir," but bellowed again, "Let me see your registration and license."

I complied. He took it back to his car, and in a few minutes he returned and said, without explanation or apology, that I could go. Of course, everything had checked out. He could have ascertained that without pulling me over. All he needed to do was to call in my license plate number. Now, I pose the question to White America, would you, at age eighty-two, dressed in a suit and tie, driving an "old man's car" home from church, be pulled over? The sense of freedom that you have, perhaps without even realizing it, must be enjoyed by all Americans.

We must emphatically declare, Black lives matter.

Since my graduation from Bluefield State College in 1954, I have sung the praises of my alma mater. I had left home a boy of seventeen and returned a true man. Let me stress that all that I am and all that I ever hope to be I owe to Bluefield State College. I was inspired by my professors. Their teaching and modeling convinced me that I could be an agent of change. When I left BSC, I believed I could change the world. I still believe that I can, and I work every day to make it happen. Bluefield State is a historically Black college (HBCU). Concerns have been raised for the last fifty years that the school is losing its heritage as a teacher's college and Black institution. I addressed this issue at the National Bluefield State Alumni Reunion in 1984:

> If we save historically Black colleges and universities, we save the Black family. If we save the Black family, we save Black communities. If we save Black communities, we save America, because she desperately needs not only our past contributions but the great potential we possess for the future. Bluefield State prepares its graduates well. Some are educators, doctors, lawyers and politicians. Nationally, 70 percent of all Black college graduates in this nation are from Black colleges, including 75 percent of Black military officers, 80 percent of Black federal judges and 85 percent of Black doctors. And, although Black colleges comprise only 5 percent of higher education in this country, they graduate almost 50 percent of Blacks at the baccalaureate level.

I shared my opinion again in a letter to the editor of the *Bluefield Daily Telegraph,* some thirty-four years later, in 2018. It referred to the apparent apathetic leadership in the area and in the City of Bluefield, who seemingly did not understand the importance of BSC. The City of Bluefield will suffer economically and in many other ways without a successful Bluefield State College. They were placing blame on the current president for the school's problems. That president, Dr. Marsha Krotseng, the first female president, had foresight enough to plan for on-campus housing and begin online classes. I will always be grateful for the actions taken by Dr. Krotseng. Her successor, Dr. Robin Capehart, moved ahead with those plans. I suggested that we work together with the City of Bluefield, school leaders, and alumni members to resolve issues such as the recruitment of students, lack of overnight housing and food services in the area, the absence of dorms, the lack of a football program, and the lack of pride in Bluefield State College. The cooperation between BSC and the community, including the City of Bluefield, has brought successes as they continue to work together more closely, beginning this process even before my letter.

Today, legalized public segregation is absent, but the circumstances of low-income youth in many of America's urban areas remain much the same as they were decades ago. Many are locked into a geographic area, an economic status, and a life without the opportunities that exist in other areas. When Woody Holton, son of Virginia's governor, was accosted in 1973 by young boys in Richmond not much older than himself, a bad situation was made better by recognizing the needs of low-income youth. They could not be ignored and wished away. Those same types of young people, three generations later, still exist in our country.

The "squeegee kids" of Baltimore cannot be ignored and wished away. These children approach cars at stoplights, walking between stopped cars looking for a nod from drivers permitting them to wash the windows with hand-held squeegee tools. They expect payment from the driver. Drivers are becoming annoyed and fearful of reported aggression. A car window was broken, a driver showed a firearm, a ten-year-old was hit by a car.

"Would y'all rather us sell drugs?" kids ask. The poverty and inequality that drives youngsters into the medians is not being addressed. They are the responsibility of us all. We need every element of the community involved: parents, social services agencies, and educational institutions. The business community should take the lead and partner with the city, churches, and others. These teenagers need opportunities and a sense that someone cares. Let's create a teenage job corps on a larger scale in Baltimore. As Woody said then, and it holds true today, "we can pay a little today or a lot more later."

Having served five presidents of the United States in sixty-five countries around the world, I consider myself to be a true American patriot. Whenever I hear songs such as "The Star-Spangled Banner" and "America the Beautiful" or recite the Pledge of Allegiance, I get teary-eyed. These are symbols of what we want America to be. However, we must realize that as a nation, we have not achieved true equality for all our citizens.

Millions of us have refused to break, we have fought back, using every tool available. My intention in sharing my life story has never been to brag but rather to inspire young Black Americans to not give in but to rise and succeed. Grateful for my hard-earned opportunities, I, along with millions of Black Americans, have competed with White America, and we have more than measured up. In many ways, we surpassed the expectations of all, even with the obstacles placed in our paths. I challenge White America to remove the obstacles, to remove the knees on our necks. You are holding America back. We have been reminded once again by a pandemic that points out the racial disparities of America and by the chilling racist murder of George Floyd, one of many that must be addressed by White America. When are you going to realize that Black lives do matter? When that happens, America can lift her voice and sing together in harmony. It can begin with a simple, peaceful revolutionary act. Let us join Colin Kaepernick and take a knee. Then, as one America, patriots all, let us rise and go to work eradicating bigotry, hatred, and prejudice in our land. Let's change this for future generations of Americans. Let us unite our nation. To do less is simply ignoring reality.

APPENDIX

Speeches, Interview, and Honors

REDISCOVERING AMERICA

Speech delivered by William B. Robertson before the United States Jaycees, Pick-Durant Hotel, Flint, Michigan, August 12, 1970

We have just entered a new decade—the 1970s. As we look back at the past decade, the 1960s, we wonder what the 1970s will bring. During the 1960s, we saw political assassinations; we saw our cities going up in flames; we saw Black against White; we saw our youngsters turn to drugs; and we found ourselves involved in a war in a faraway land, Vietnam. Are these indications of things which we will find in the 1970s?

I maintain that the 1970s must be the decade in which Americans will rediscover or discover America for what she really is and for what she really stands. And I say rediscover because many of us have forgotten why America was founded, and many of us have never really discovered it. So, the two key words are "rediscovery" and "discover."

We can trace America's beginning back to the Renaissance. During that period in Europe when people began to come alive, when there was a revival, a new birth of learning, people began to understand that the society of that day was not offering them the freedom which every person expected, which every person needed. And because of this Renaissance, we found that people began to learn to read, and to wonder what was across the seas.

After this, many explorers came to the New World. The Spaniards continued to come to Central and South America; they went out into the great southwestern section of what is now the United States. The French came to the New World and settled in the Mississippi Valley region. Basically, they were there to trap animals and carry their furs back to Europe to be sold at market. But in 1588, a significant event happened—the Spanish Armada was defeated by the English Sea Dogs and England became mistress of the seas as she began to send her explorers to the New World. John Cabot laid claim to all the land from Newfoundland and all down the Atlantic seacoast for England. Sir Walter Raleigh helped to establish a colony which became known as the Lost Colony.

But, in 1607, the first permanent English settlement began in America at Jamestown, Virginia. Things did not always go well for this settlement, but a strong leader came upon the scene. This strong leader, in the person of Captain John Smith, held the new colony together, and it survived.

In 1619, three important events happened in the Jamestown colony: women were brought from England to serve as brides for the settlers; the House of Burgesses was set up, which became a forerunner of the Virginia General Assembly; and, in that same year, twenty Black people were brought from Africa, and, ultimately, the evil institution of slavery became a reality in these United States.

In 1620, we found the Pilgrims and the Puritans coming to America, going to Plymouth Rock, Massachusetts, and yes, the English continued to come. They went down into North Carolina, South Carolina, and Georgia. We found that the Swedes went up into Delaware, the Catholics went into Maryland; we found that the English went into what is now New York, and continuously went up into the New England section of our country, and before we knew it, we had the thirteen original colonies.

But all was not well. The English found themselves at odds with the French, and in 1756, we went to war with France. This war in America was known as the French and Indian War, and in Europe, it was known as the Seven Years' War. In 1763, we were rid of the French menace. Yes, we were victorious as far as this war was concerned.

Again, dark clouds hovered over the original thirteen colonies, and we found the trouble this time arose from the mother country herself, England. The mother country felt we should pay the expenses incurred in the war with France. England began to levy taxes upon the colonies. There was a Stamp Act, a Molasses Act, a Sugar Act, and people in the colonies began to wonder why they should pay these taxes. Patrick Henry, the man who became known as the "tongue of the American Revolution," stood up and expressed it well when he said: "Taxation without representation is tyranny. Forbid it, Almighty God! I know not what course others may take, but as for me, give me liberty or give me death!" The battle cry had been sounded. In 1770, in Boston, we found the Boston Massacre took place, and one of the first to fall during the Boston Massacre was a Black man by the name of Crispus Attucks. There is a shrine dedicated to this man on the Boston Commons.

In 1773, members of the Boston Colony, dressed as Indians, boarded an English ship and threw thousands of dollars' worth of tea into the harbor. In 1775, there were the battles at Lexington and Concord. And not only were there White men there, but we found a Black man, Peter Salem, fighting alongside his White brothers, the White members of the colony, protecting those places against the Englishmen, and yes, they were victorious.

In 1776, July Fourth, Thomas Jefferson wrote the famous words, "We hold these truths to be self-evident, that all men are created equal; that they are endowed by their Creator with certain unalienable rights, that among these are life, liberty, and the pursuit of happiness."

Yes, we had declared ourselves free and independent from Great Britain. But this was not enough, for then we had to go out onto the battlefield and prove there that we were free and independent. This is what we did. Not only did we have White colonists fighting but also Black colonists fighting alongside them to see to it that this freedom and independence came into being.

The history books of America have failed to tell the White child and the Black child that the White man and the Black man fought together to bring about this victory. We achieved this in 1781, when Cornwallis surrendered to Washington at Yorktown. We found many people coming to this nation to help us between the years 1776 and 1781. We found a German by the name of Von Steuben who came to help; a person who came from Poland named Count Pulaski, and yes, a Lafayette from France. We found men who believed in freedom who came to this nation to see to it that the thirteen colonies would emerge victorious. And again, Black men and White men fought for the survival of this country, for their freedom, for their independence, and it did come, in 1781. But once the war was over, there was nothing to really hold the thirteen colonies together. We were still thirteen separate colonies. We drew up the Articles of Confederation, but we found that these articles were not strong enough to bind us together. In 1787, a Constitutional Convention was called in Philadelphia, and representatives from the colonies went there in order to draw up the Constitution.

There was a floor fight, and it seemed as if the Constitutional Convention would fail. But a wise old gentleman named Benjamin Franklin brought about the Great Compromise, which stated that there would be two Houses of Government, that every state would have two representatives who would represent their states in the Upper House, which would be known as the Senate. On the basis of population, representatives would come from every state, and this saved the Constitutional Convention, and the Constitution came into being. The Bill of Rights, preceded by a preamble, came into being. It stated that, "We, the people of the United States, in order to form a more perfect union, establish justice, insure domestic tranquility, provide for the common defense, promote the general welfare and secure the blessings of liberty to ourselves and our posterity, do ordain and establish this Constitution for the United States of America." We decided that no longer would there be a king in this country, that we would have a president who would be elected by the people. In 1789, George Washington became the first president of these United States. In 1803, under the leadership of President Thomas Jefferson, our country increased in size when we purchased the Louisiana Territory from France for the sum of $15 million. This purchase now includes approximately thirteen states.

But again, dark clouds hovered. Great Britain had not really realized that America had won the War for Independence, and a second War of Independence had to be fought. It was known as the War of 1812. It began in 1809 because the English were beginning to take men off American ships and make them serve in the English navy. We went to war again, and once again, we were victorious.

One of the most significant things that came out of this was when a young man named Francis Scott Key was carried aboard an English ship off the coast of Baltimore at Fort McHenry. Through the night, as he was held captive by the British, the ship bombarded the fort, and he wondered what the outcome would be. Would the American flag still be flying the next morning, or would the Union Jack be flying? Through the night he kept wondering to himself, how will the battle go, what will tomorrow bring? As the dawn came about and the fog lifted and the smoke cleared, he saw a tattered American flag still flying. He was thrilled and took a quill and paper in his hands and began to write, "O, say can you see by the dawn's early light . . ." We could see coming into formation the words that make up the national anthem that we, both Black and White, so proudly sing today. Andrew Jackson, in 1815, with Black and White men fighting together, not realizing that the War of 1812 was over, fought the Battle of New Orleans. They were victorious.

During 1836, the cry was, "Save the Alamo!" There were David Crockett, Jim Bowie, and Black and White men who fought Santa Anna at the Alamo. Mexicans overran the Alamo in San Antonio, but the cry went up, "Remember the Alamo, remember the Alamo." We found that in 1845 we defeated the Mexicans, and in 1848 Texas became a state.

Dark clouds still hovered above the American scene. America was being torn apart over tariffs and the issue of slavery. In 1861, with the founding of Fort Sumter in Charleston Harbor, the Civil War began, and this war was the bloodiest that this nation has ever known. Brother fought against brother, section against section. We said to ourselves that this would never happen again in these United States. In the year 1863, at the dedication of a cemetery in Gettysburg, the president of the United States, Abraham Lincoln, uttered these words, "That this nation, under God, should have a new birth of freedom, and that government of the people, by the people, and for the people, shall not perish from this earth." During the same year, the Emancipation Proclamation was issued. It said that Negroes were no longer to be slaves. The war ended in 1865, but in the same year, Abraham Lincoln, the man who was to bring us together, was assassinated by a half-crazed actor, John Wilkes Booth. We went into a period of Reconstruction that saw our nation come together again. At the same time, the Transcontinental Railroad was built, and we found many other people coming to America. The Chinese came to work to see that this railroad came into being. Yes, the great immigration period began. The people began to come from other parts of Europe: the Irish came, the Germans came, and the Poles. And we became, truly, the melting-pot nation.

In 1898, we went to war once again. This time when the battleship USS *Maine* was blown up in Havana Harbor, we found Teddy Roosevelt with Black and White Americans riding up San Juan Hill. Again, we were victorious as far as the Spanish-American War was concerned.

In 1917, we again found ourselves at war. This time it was in France, fighting the Germans. The American doughboys were fighting under the leadership of Pershing, and at home, everyone was singing, "Over there, over there, we won't come back 'til it's over, over there." The song was written by George M. Cohan. We didn't come back until it was over, over there. Black men and White men, Black Americans and White Americans, fighting together, to see to it that France became secure. This was to be the war to end all wars.

Yet, twenty-five years later, we found ourselves at war again, this time with the Japanese, who attacked Pearl Harbor on December 7, 1941. There a great hero came into being, a Black man by the name of Dorie Miller, who was a cook. At this particular time, that was all that a Black man could be in the United States Navy. He came up from the kitchen and manned a machine gun and shot down a Japanese plane; a Black man who had not been trained to do this type of work, who could only wait tables but still showed his skill and courage. Yes, we fought the Second World War, Black and White together, and we saw to it that we were victorious as we won the war against Japan, Germany, and Italy, and we saw that this was the war to end all wars, but it was not.

A few years later, we found ourselves in a faraway place known as Korea. That was the Twenty-Fourth Infantry Division, composed of Black men and later integrated, which won fame for itself. Again, we were victorious to a certain extent because this was supposed to have been polite action that was not officially declared a war.

Now we find ourselves in Vietnam, and while we in the United States find ourselves at odds with each other, one race against another, we find our boys, Black and White, fighting and dying side by side in the rice paddies in Vietnam. How stupid can we get? Why can't we live together as Americans, side by side, and not think in terms of whether we are White or Black? Why must our cities go up in smoke? Why is it that one American treats another American as if he is a second-class citizen? Why can't we live in this country as Americans because it has taken all of us to build this country to the greatness that we find in it today? This greatness becomes even greater once we realize that we need each other, that we are interdependent. There is no place in this nation today for division, Black against White, young against old. We must come together as Americans and forget about the old prejudices that we once harbored.

Yes, we must discover or rediscover America and realize why it was founded, why it was settled. People in Europe realized that they were not enjoying the freedoms that human beings should enjoy, and this is the very essence of why American came into being. Yet, on the other hand, we are still saying to certain segments of our population that you don't belong, that you are not like us; you must live where we say you must live; you must take the mediocre jobs. I say, we must rediscover America and realize how this country came into being and why it came into being.

That is how you and I, as Jaycees, can be of great value to our country. As young men of action, we can bring America together by opening our doors of membership to every young man so that he might learn leadership training through community development.

Doesn't one line of our creed state that the brotherhood of man transcends the sovereignty of nations? Yet, many of our chapters still have segregated clauses in their constitutions. Young men are going to lead one way or another. Do we want them to lead through the Jaycees or through other means? We have grave responsibilities. I am afraid that there are many of us who need to rediscover America. The Jaycees should be for every young man between twenty-one and thirty-five.

Once we do this, we will find that America will become an even greater nation, and we can look back to the words of Thomas Jefferson and truly say with real conviction, "We hold these truths to be self-evident, that all men are created equal; that they are endowed by their Creator with certain unalienable rights, that among these are life, liberty, and the pursuit of happiness." Then, surely, America will have become the land of the free and the home of the brave.

PRESENTATION BY WILLIAM B. ROBERTSON, MEMBER, PRESIDENT'S COMMITTEE ON MENTAL RETARDATION, AND DIRECTOR, OFFICE OF CONSUMER AFFAIRS

Delivered at the Annual Conference of the National Association for the Mentally Retarded (now the Arc of the United States), Las Vegas, Nevada, October 21, 1975

Ladies and Gentlemen,
I bring greetings from the President's Committee on Mental Retardation.

The Declaration of Independence and the Constitution of the United States epitomize the so-called American dream. Yet, the words emanating from these documents have not reached all Americans with the connotations they should. They have not become a reality for those who are not truly in the mainstream. If we wish to reduce the 3 percent figure as far as mental retardation is concerned, we must speak as advocates for the exceptional children who live in the other America, the America which many would love to dismiss as not existing.

We must speak as advocates for Chicano children who are relegated to the barrios of the Southwest and other parts of this country. We must speak as advocates for Black children in Harlem and the other ghettos of America. We must speak as advocates for Puerto Ricans who reside in Connecticut, New York, and other places in America—those children who find their fathers the last to be hired and the first to be fired. We must speak as advocates for Indian children who see suicides and feel hunger. We must speak as advocates for Appalachian White children and those who live in our cities and the rural backwoods of America. These children fall into the category of being disadvantaged economically and socially. This indicates they are exceptional.

If normality means residing in a ranch home with green grass and flowers growing, a father who dresses in a business suit and drives to work with his briefcase by his side, a mother who either works in the home with a white starched apron or works at a skilled job—then surely those groups just described are exceptional. They are exceptional in other ways. Many are in special-education classes for the educable mentally retarded. Test scores indicate they are below average in intelligence.

In addition to the constant fight for survival which middle America tends to ignore, members of minority groups have cultures in which lifestyles, habits, customs, and languages deviate from the so-called norm.

Yet, the larger culture decides through testing—testing geared to take in experiences, habits, customs, and language of that particular group which is to be the absolute for all. Chicano children speak Spanish while the tests are in English. Teachers will tell those youngsters if they want to do well, they must learn to speak English. Spanish is spoken in their neighborhoods so these boys and girls speak two languages while the vast majority of teachers only speak English. Suppose these children were encouraged to retain Spanish while being prepared well to use English. Would there be as many Chicano children in special-education classes if tests were written in Spanish and questions centered around culture known by these youngsters?

Many Black children in ghettos do not take tests well. Present reading endeavors do not remind them of the environments in which they live. The question is—would there be as many of these youngsters in special-education classes if the language, customs, and experiences they are accustomed to were brought into focus?

Indian children asked on tests to describe such things as subways may never have seen a subway. The reservation is a way of life. There are few books in the home. A television set could be a luxury. There is constant hunger. Many of these children are labeled mentally retarded.

These are the conditions under which many of our children labor. These conditions exist in America—"The land of the free and home of the brave." These conditions exist in a land where men and women are known to fight and die in the name of freedom—in a land where Black men, White men, Brown men, Red men, Yellow men, have let their blood run together in order for us to call ourselves free.

These conditions exist in a land where Chicano children know little about their ancestors at the Alamo or the great deeds they perform today. They only know that they are abused—they are made fun of by Anglos. They must be villains, and the Anglos must be the good guys. Isn't that the way it is on television and in the movies?

Many Black children don't know of the great contributions made by their ancestors and the ones Blacks continue to make. They are only made to realize that Blacks commit crimes. They are told that they are lazy and shiftless. Isn't that the true picture of Blacks in America? Indian children know little about their ancestors who helped to save the Jamestown Colony by teaching the colonists how to cultivate crops. They know little about the fact that their people built the first apartment houses in America. They only know that the Indian was a savage and the White cavalry had to subdue him. Isn't that the way the Indian is looked upon?

Appalachian Whites know little about the free spirit of the mountain people—their link to Daniel Boone and the westward movement. They only know of the moonshiners, of illegitimate children, and the lazy good-for-nothing hillbilly. Isn't that the way it is with the mountain people?

Is it any wonder that these children rebel against the majority culture while at the same time begin to question in a very negative way, without realizing it, their own rich cultures?

Is this the way in which the majority culture hopes to maintain what it considers superiority over the so-called subcultures? I do not believe this is the case. For more and more the way of the future is becoming clear.

America is a nation of cultures—not a melting pot but rather a cultural pluralism. Our system has betrayed our minority cultures. Especially has the educational system been a betrayal because it has not recognized all cultures in such a way that greater respect for each other has come into being. This educational system has penalized those who have not measured up to the so-called norm. Special-education classes have become the dumping grounds for these youngsters, and ultimately, many will drop out of school. We also are being failed and suspended in alarming numbers throughout the country.

The big cry emanating across this land is HOW LONG? How long can you ignore us? The answer comes back, loudly and clearly, NOT LONG. Not long, not long because we are not going to let you! Ladies and gentlemen, we must join them as their advocates. We must echo their cry through positive action—not long because we are not going to let you.

U.S. WANTS AN END TO APARTHEID

Address by William B. Robertson, Deputy Assistant Secretary for African Affairs, before the International Conference Against Apartheid at Ebenezer Baptist Church, Atlanta, Georgia, January 19, 1986; published by the United States Department of State, Bureau of Public Affairs, Office of Public Communication, Editorial Division, Washington, D.C., February 1986

Mrs. [Coretta Scott] King, Bishop [Desmond] Tutu, Major General Joseph Garba, distinguished pulpit associates, members of this great church, ladies and gentlemen from Atlanta and around the world, my brothers and sisters. I am honored to be with you on this red-letter date, this historic occasion. We gather on the eve of a nationwide celebration to reflect upon the life and work of a truly great human being—Dr. Martin Luther King Jr. Dr. King, an American, belongs to the world. As Secretary Edwin Stanton said of Abraham Lincoln, "Now he belongs to the Ages." So it is with Dr. Martin Luther King Jr.

We owe Dr. King a great debt. This integrated audience is a testimony to him. I owe the position I hold to Dr. King, as do many of you here today and others around the nation and world.

We must struggle to conquer those who would withhold freedom from any group, anywhere in the world because of race, creed, or gender, whether it be in the United States or South Africa; that is what he would have us do.

Bishop Tutu, we owe you our gratitude because you espouse the concepts of freedom and equality for men, women, and children everywhere. We ask you to keep on keeping on.

I was in South Africa last month, and on a Sunday morning in that land, spoke before a church congregation—people who had endured the vicious system of apartheid all week and had come to receive the spiritual nourishment needed to make it through another week. They brought their babies to be baptized that morning; their pre-teen daughters wore white dresses and sons wore suits and ties for confirmation. What a moving experience to speak before these people of color who came to present their children to God and to receive Holy Communion.

As I looked out at that audience, I saw my mother; I saw my grandmother; I saw my father; I saw my brothers and sisters; I saw my friends and neighbors. The miles made no difference. The distance from America meant nothing. The people in that church wanted then and want now the same thing that people everywhere desire—they want freedom.

The Quest for Freedom

Much has been written these past few months about the situation in South Africa. Certainly, the conscience of this nation, the world, and South Africa has been alerted to the critical nature of events in that republic by those who initially started the protests at the embassy in Washington. This concept of bringing attention to that which is clearly wrong and needing reform is one of the purest forms of our democratic system here in America.

Yet, our concerns for those who are outside the mainstream in that country, the disenfranchised, the pass bearers, those who are separated from the full family structure because of a rigid system of racism and segregation and other acts which render them to be below that of even second-class citizenship actually began hundreds of years ago in Europe during the Renaissance—a period of revival, a time of awakening. This was the period when men and women found themselves lying flat on the ground with the heels of other men and women, of so-called higher status in life, squarely in their faces. These disadvantaged people began to cry that human beings are not supposed to live in that manner. They understood that they should walk upright and be able to determine their own destinies. Out of this desire for human dignity, out of this search for collective and individual freedom, America was founded. It continued to manifest itself during the pre–Revolutionary War period, when strong leaders such as Thomas Jefferson, Patrick Henry, and Benjamin Franklin came to the forefront, and in a struggle for independence we became free and independent men and women.

The quest for freedom was again demonstrated by Blacks in America from the time slaves were introduced in this country through the height of the civil rights era to the present. Martin Luther King's "I Have a Dream" oration is a testimony to the fact that Americans desire freedom here at home and abroad for those who understand that there is grave responsibility for possessing it.

U.S. Message to South Africa

Therefore, no one should confuse or misread the message coming out of America today for it is a loud and clear one. This message to South Africa is "end apartheid."

The American public is crying, "end apartheid." The Congress of the United States is crying, "end apartheid." The president of our nation is crying, "end apartheid." Hopefully, Pretoria fully understands that there is no disagreement relative to this position.

This administration has gone on record indicating its disdain for a policy which relegates approximately twenty-three million people, a majority, basically to a status of serfdom—this population which cries for freedom, this population which wants nothing more than to be free men and women in their native land.

For this reason, the administration has indicated that the United States will not abandon those who suffer under this system on a daily basis. We'll not fold our tents and go away. We shall continue to use what influence we have in South Africa to bring an end to apartheid.

Working with groups such as you, those meeting in other parts of our country, those in nations around the world, and, yes, those working in South Africa for positive change, Martin's dream will live in South Africa— apartheid will end.

Each day brings additional news from South Africa—more people have been killed; the press is denied access to those situations which should be reported; arrests have been made. Yes, these are the negatives. Yet, every day people are inquiring, what can we do to assist? How might we play a role in bringing about positive reform?

That is why we have assembled at this time, because it means more involvement in order to improve the lives of Black South Africans. We should and can be involved in such things as:

- Helping Blacks in South Africa, which is the goal of our own education and trade union programs, which will be expanded under the president's executive order.

- Using our colleges and universities to train Black South Africans in management, business, and technology. We hope every institution of higher learning will participate in a program of this nature. Black colleges and universities have played major roles in training those who have been in leadership positions in Africa. We now hope they will continue this distinguished work in preparing South Africans who will be the backbone of not only constructive change but also the making of a new South Africa along with others who understand that this must happen. This also suggests that faculties and students work on projects in South Africa which will directly benefit the Black population of that republic.

- Helping the neighbors in the southern African region as they struggle to survive and develop in a very difficult part of the world.

Several weeks ago, I sat with Vice President [George H. W.] Bush as he held talks with representatives from one of the countries in southern Africa. The vice president used this as an opportunity to indicate how strongly opposed the United States is to apartheid. The delegates voiced their approval for America's stand but indicated that their land-locked country was really caught in the middle. They, too, were opposed to apartheid but really were restricted from voicing disapproval strongly because they would be subject to retaliation from South Africa. Also, they felt that sanctions would be harmful to them for the following reasons: if imposed, South Africa would take care of its own and possibly put into effect such economic curbs as not allowing goods to flow to shops in that country. Roads could not be used. Its ports would not be available. Members of the workforce going to South Africa would be sent back to the country. Electricity would be cut off, and the litany continued. Eight or nine countries in the region have their economics tied to what happens in South Africa. If South Africa goes down the drain economically, so do these countries. If it does, an entire region on an already impoverished continent is lost.

We recommend using the Sullivan principles [developed by Rev. Leon Sullivan to promote corporate social responsibility] via our private sector to create a climate in South Africa, which will indicate that Blacks and Whites can work together on an equal basis, and utilizing this approach to illustrate that equal employment is good business, that equal pay brings about greater production, that open housing creates a sense of partnership, that training programs and employment mobility lead to a strengthened workplace.

We need to add to our activities in order to assist Black South Africa to increase those skills needed to perform in a new South Africa—one that more readily reflects the racial makeup of that republic. Education and business development must be at the top of that list.

Economically, we cannot leave South Africa in shambles. We must stay but always prod for change. We must see that the environment constantly signals change. We must ask all progressive South Africans—Black, White, colored, Asian—to join hands with us as we jointly seek positive reform. Our aim must always be that of bringing South Africa to its senses, not to its knees. It must function on the world market when apartheid is dismantled. We must see that it enters this arena with strength.

Appeal to the South African Government

In closing, there is a message for the South African government. There is still time. You must help to save South Africa. You must take the initiative to bring about positive reform. Lift the emergency. Release Nelson Mandela and other political prisoners. Let Black South Africans select their representatives who will go to the negotiating table. Get on with the job of unifying South Africa.

The United States and, virtually, the world, are saying to you, in the words of the old Black spiritual: "Let my people go." And, in doing so, a strong, vibrant, new South Africa will come into being with all of its people working together. This South Africa and its neighbors will be the envy of every region in the world. We can then paraphrase the words of James Weldon Johnson:

We have lifted our voices to sing;
We have heard earth and heaven sing;
We have been true to our God;
We have been true to our native land;
We have cared and shared;
Today victory is won.

OPPOSITION TO SANCTIONS TRIES TO KEEP U.S. FOOT IN THE DOOR

San Diego Union Interview, July 27, 1986

The Reagan administration believes complete isolation of South Africa would end hope of U.S. leverage there and, as a result, would extend apartheid, William B. Robertson told *San Diego Union* editors.
Robertson is deputy assistant secretary of state for African affairs.

Q: South Africa seems to be careening towards civil and tribal war, and things have gone almost beyond the point of no return. Do I have the wrong impression?

A: I do not feel that it has gone beyond the point of no return. That's the reason it is vitally important for American businesses and other entities to remain in South Africa, so we can use the leverage available through their presence to bring about the type of negotiations that will usher in a post-apartheid South Africa in which Blacks, Whites, coloreds, Indians, etc., will engage in a shared power, a truly multi-racial, democratic society.

Q: We've tried to exert this leverage before, and it doesn't seem to do much good. What makes you optimistic that it will be effective now?

A: There have been some gains in the last five years—for example, the abolition of the pass laws in South Africa just recently—that I think can be attributed to efforts put forth by the American business community. But I am convinced that if we pull out of South Africa, if we bring about sanctions, we doom Black South Africans to entrenchment of that evil apartheid system for another 15, 20, 25 years. What we have done is to back away, we have become involved in the internal situation there. I hear in what President Botha and others say, "Bring on your sanctions, but we're tired of you pecking away at us. We're tired of you making determinations as to what's supposed to take place in South Africa." We need to continue to peck away, to continue to do that which is necessary to confront that government that we want to change.

Q: Would you say the situation today in South Africa is worse or better than five years ago?

A: I think expectations are higher today than five years ago on the part of the Black community. This has brought about a greater degree of fear in the White community. But when we look at that White community, I think we have been able to solicit the Afrikaners. Afrikaners, especially the young ones, are beginning to ask what is this thing they call apartheid? And why cannot there be change? On the other side are the right wing and Botha and others who see sanctions as giving them a rallying cry to bring Afrikaners together.

Q: If the U.S. policy of constructive engagement hasn't produced the successes that many hoped or predicted, and the administration remains opposed to sanctions, what's the alternative to what we are doing now?

A: Since 1981, when the Reagan administration came into office, more has been done than in perhaps the ten years prior to that. But the alternative to what is taking place is the isolation of South Africa, and I think that's worse than what we are engaged in. At this point, we have an opportunity, some leverage, through which we can address the government there, some leverage in terms of working with the people to bring about an end to apartheid. But if we isolate South Africa again, I am convinced that we would entrench apartheid.

Q: There seems to be two countries in the forefront against sanctions, England and the United States. England is facing a very serious problem in that Prime Minister Thatcher apparently is having a confrontation with the queen, who doesn't want to see the Commonwealth break up over this issue. Might we reach a point where the United States is isolated and Mrs. Thatcher might have to give in on sanctions?

A: I see the United States and Great Britain standing together. What we don't want to do is isolate South Africa. Not only are we talking in terms of what sanctions will do to the economy of South Africa, what it would do to the unemployment rate in Great Britain or the jobs that will be lost in the United States, but we're also talking about the whole southern Africa region. I was in Lesotho last December and saw women lined up at the banks on a Friday morning. I asked my colleague, a citizen of that country, if these women had enough money to be either depositing or withdrawing it. He said they were mothers and wives of men who work in the mines in South Africa and were there to receive money withheld from the pay of those men. This money makes up 50 percent of the gross national product of Lesotho. Let's say we impose sanctions. South Africa then can say, "We have to take care of our own; we cannot bring into our workforce those from Lesotho and the other countries in that region." That means Lesotho and the other countries will be economically destroyed. What about the Botswanans; what about the Malawis? This is a region in which sanctions would add eight or ten countries to the lists of demolished economies in a continent that is already economically devastated.

Q: I think it might be useful at this point to define the word sanction, which is a very broad term. You're talking about complete disinvestment. Aren't there measures that the United States can take short of ultimate disinvestment such as contacts with Black leaders in South Africa, reducing representations and so forth?

A: We are already in contact with Black leaders in South Africa. Let me indicate that Herman Nickel, our ambassador to South Africa, has done an outstanding job under very trying circumstances in that republic.

Q: Is there any possibility of a meeting, say, between President Reagan and Oliver Tambo of the African National Congress?

A: I think we are going to see additional meetings between U.S. governmental officials and the ANC. We have met with the ANC in the past.

Q: What is the Reagan administration's view of the political alignment of the ANC? Is it a communist organization or one that if it seized power in South Africa would operate a Marxist-style, one-party state?

A: There are those who would espouse democracy, those who are socialistic in their thinking and there might be some who are thinking in terms of Marxism within the ANC. But the ANC has been in existence for a fairly long time and has been moderate over the years. I think critics who lean toward the communists actually are using that as an excuse to not do the types of things that are necessary and most of that talk comes from South Africa. I do not see the ANC as a true threat in terms of communism. But let me quickly add that violence from the government or being perpetrated by the ANC is something we abhor and if we isolate South Africa, that means we can't work with ANC through educational programs, the development of Black businesses, the whole concept of working with legal aid groups. Also, if the ANC becomes isolated, what does it do? There is the possibility that it will look elsewhere and that is something we would not like to see take place.

Q: Aren't they already looking elsewhere?

A: I think they are looking in a number of directions. If I happen to be in a river and think I am drowning, it doesn't make much difference to me who is going to save me. In that sense, I want to make certain that I am in South Africa representing the United States so I can do the kind of rescuing that needs to be done. If you pull me out of the country, I can't play the role of lifeguard.

Q: Is there any indication that you can give us on possible release of Nelson Mandela?

A: There isn't. But we called, and continue to call for the release of Nelson Mandela and other political prisoners. It is my opinion that the key to the future of South Africa rests with Mandela. If he is allowed to remain a prisoner and something happens to him there, that sends a negative signal to the Black community. Mandela has to be released from prison and he and other Black leaders chosen by the Black community must sit at a conference table with White leaders of that government, plus those who are colored, Indian, etc. and hammer out a post-apartheid South Africa.

Q: His death would have a terrible effect?

A: It would have a horrible effect on the situation now and the prospects for peace and unity.

Q: President Botha has said he will release Mandela if the ANC renounces violence. Do you see this happening?

A: No. Nelson Mandela cannot renounce violence because then he loses his credibility with his ANC colleagues and others in the Black community. Mandela has to be released without restrictions. Mandela, in my estimation, is a very visionary individual who not only can pull the ANC together, but can pull the Black community together. If this afternoon it were announced that apartheid had ended, I think you would find disarray and jockeying for position in the Black community of South Africa. Mandela has to be the one to galvanize the Black community.

Q: Is there any other leader who could unify the Black community?

A: I think at this particular time, Mandela is the leader.

Q: Would he get any support from Chief Buthelezi?

A: I think we're going to see a type of cooperation between Mandela and Buthelezi. Truly, these are the giants in the Black community in South Africa and despite what we often read and hear, they have been colleagues in the past and I think they can work together.

Q: Is the U.S. State Department able to maintain any sort of contact with Mandela?

A: We are in touch with the AFC. That brings us in touch with Mandela.

Q: Does the experience in Zimbabwe slow things up in South Africa? Is that making the White leaders in South Africa more nervous about moving ahead?

A: I think it slows things up, but at the same time it offers a signal in terms of what positive things could happen in South Africa. There were White Rhodesians who were fearful and left the country, but now we see a trend of Whites coming back to Zimbabwe. There are those who say sanctions helped to bring about the independence of Zimbabwe. However, it was some fourteen, fifteen years after sanctions came into effect before Zimbabwe gained freedom.

Q: Some people believe the White minority in South Africa will never accept, without war, a system in which there is "one-man, one-vote." Many of these people believe that the only workable choice is some sort of power-sharing federation in which apartheid is dismantled. Do you see that as the best possible alternative to either continuation of apartheid or a suicidal civil war?

A: I'm not so certain that we have "one-man, one-vote" in this country, thinking in terms of the way the electoral college might be set up. But either power is going to be shared in South Africa or there is going to be no power to share. There has to be this sole recognition that the government will be dominated by Black South Africans, but with acceptance of rights of minorities. I spoke at East Carolina University several months ago and the question was posed to me [whether] I would have talked in these terms to American slaves 125 years ago. It hit me right in the gut, but my response was, if I could've talked with slaves in the American South 125–130 years ago, I would've said that slaves must be freed in this country, but, hopefully, that could come without the Civil War. The analogy is that Blacks in South Africa must be free, must be full-fledged, voting citizens of the republic but without civil war. Blacks are free in this country, but remembrance of the Civil War still exists—there are pockets where that war is still being fought. It takes hundreds of years for such wounds to heal.

Q: You don't see a federated state as opposed to a military state?

A: I just want to see a situation in South Africa where people are free to move and live and work where they want to live and work, and an economic system that will allow that. I think it is for South Africans to determine for themselves exactly what they think post-apartheid South Africa should be all about.

Q: The South African ambassador to the United States is consistently saying that the Botha government wants to do away with apartheid and is moving toward greater political participation, etc. Is that just a public relations gambit or are they, in their own way, sincere?

A: I think Black South Africans would say these efforts on the part of the government are too little, too late. If we talk with the ambassador to the United States from South Africa and many of the officials in the South African government, they are wondering why we are not jumping up and down with joy in terms of the types of initiatives that they have taken. But again, what they must understand is that the height of expectations has grown tremendously, and a snail-like approach is not going to be well accepted by the Black community or by the world community.

Q: If Botha and Mandela were, eyeball to eyeball, to negotiate a new formula, how long might the transition take?

A: If we look at that situation in our own country when segregation was coming to an end, that change didn't come overnight. Last December I asked a Black citizen of South Africa who lives in Soweto if apartheid ended this evening or tomorrow morning, what differences would it make to the vast majorities of the people? He said you would see little exodus from Soweto to other parts of South Africa because the economic factors must be figured in and people feel comfortable at their homes. I would say the true effects might be felt three, four, five years down the road but what is so very important is they would understand that they have the right to do the things that are now forbidden.

Q: We don't hear much about Namibia. What is going on there?

A: We're still looking for withdrawal of South African troops there, and there could be some announcement relative to that sometime after August, also in relation to the reduction of Cuban forces in Angola.

MESSAGE FROM CAMP VIRGINIA JAYCEE COUNSELOR

October 18, 2018

To Whom It May Concern,

I have worked and volunteered at Camp Virginia Jaycee for many years, in many capacities.

That first summer in 1996 was hard. I was unskilled in working with people with disabilities. My limited experience as a camp counselor did not prepare me for that summer, but then, nothing could. I did not know that would become the basis of my career and a fundamental part of who I am. This was not my design; I was going to be a music journalist, or so I thought.

One summer became two and two became at least eight, but I've honestly lost count.

Camp Jaycee isn't just a place. It isn't the land the buildings sit on. It is sacred territory. It is the place of lifelong friendships, relationships, and growing pains. Many of us that have worked there have stayed in the field of education, recreation, counselors, therapists, working with people that have disabilities.

In hot, long summers when we exchanged addresses and said our good-byes, we never thought there would be a point when we wouldn't be back. We made plans for reunions, promises to bring back kids and families.

Now, here we are, feeling as displaced as our campers do. I looked into a pair of sad eyes this summer, soulful eyes, as our camper said, "Camp Jaycee is home. I want to go home."

All I could say was, "I know." Because I do know.

What has happened to camp isn't right and it isn't fair. Camp Jaycee is Bill Robertson's legacy. He had a vision for camp during a time when "mentally retarded" was an acceptable term for our population. He knew our campers needed a safe space to recreate long before "safe space" became a catchword.

Times have changed, vocabulary has changed and standards have changed, but the thing that never changed about Camp Jaycee is that it always remained a traditional outdoor camping experience. In its nearly 50 years, Camp Jaycee has never significantly changed its program, never became steeped in technology or anything fancy. It has always been about the old-school, traditional camping experience: campfires, fishing, swimming, mosquito bites.

Our campers want to come back. Our staff wants to come back and introduce a new generation to the relentless humidity of a Virginia summer, to the red clay of Roanoke that never really comes out of clothes, as well as to campfires, and s'mores.

Sincerely,
Christie Thomas, CTRS

BLUEFIELD STATE COLLEGE LIBRARY REDEDICATION

President Robin Capehart, August 2019

Ladies and gentleman, today marks the kickoff of a year-long celebration of Bluefield State's 125th Anniversary, a celebration of our school's rich and vibrant heritage that will provide the inspiration for the beginning of a new year. A new era of hope, unity, and prosperity.

Today we gather together to honor an individual who truly embodies this heritage, whose achievements are remarkable and . . . whose life is genuinely inspiring. We choose to pay tribute to this alum by rededicating this building in his honor. The building that has been called the temple of learning and the observation made that learning has liberated more people than all the wars in history. Ladies and gentlemen, the man we honor today has such a passion for the importance of this building to our students that many years ago he established an endowment so future generations could use the valuable resources here to learn to build a better future and pursue and achieve success, much as he has done. I'm sure many of you here today have a memory or two of times that you spent countless hours of studying or researching or cramming for a test or just trying to find a place to satisfy an inquisitive mind. However, it doesn't escape our memories also that for decades, the designation placed upon this treasured building brought to mind a time of perhaps the greatest injustice ever put upon the students of this institution. And as such for years, many of you have been carrying a deep sorrow for the pain inflicted upon this place that has been so near and dear to your heart. Dr. Martin Luther King once stated that we should never succumb to the temptation of bitterness. And that we must accept finite disappointments but never lose infinite hope. Ladies and gentlemen, this finite disappointment of the past is over and the infinite hope that is inspired by the life and accomplishments of our honoree, shall be planted in our hearts and our minds. For as long as we continue to love and cherish this great institution, it serves as a beacon of hope and opportunity for future generations. Dr. King also said the time is always right to do what is right. Today we are doing what is right.

As most of you know, our honoree has maintained a long passionate history with his alma mater, including the times he would bring scores of students for campus visits. His storied career in the Peace Corps and service under a Virginia governor and five U.S. presidents are most remarkable, and again, inspirational.

Needless to say, we have before us a man whose life was changed by Bluefield State College, and in return he has gone out and had a significant impact on the lives of others. His legacy of service and leadership and a passion for this school is indeed exemplary, and a legacy worth our actions today.

Therefore, by the authority invested by my office, by the board of governors of Bluefield State College, we hereby dedicate the Bluefield State College library in honor of William B. Robertson; it shall now and forevermore be known as the William B. Robertson Library.

HONORS

1965	Outstanding Young Educator in Roanoke for work to prevent dropouts
1966–67	Letter of Commendation from President of Radford College for work as specialist with Head Start faculty
1967	Outstanding Young Man in Roanoke by panel of citizens
1967	One of five Outstanding Young Men in Virginia

1968 & 1969	Roanoke Jaycees, "Spark Plug of the Year" for overall Jaycee performance
1968	Roanoke Jaycees, Jaycee of the Month for all-around performance
1968	Knights of Columbus, Knight of the Month for outstanding work with monthly publications
1968	Letter of Commendation from Joseph P. Kennedy Jr. Foundation for outstanding work in the area of mental retardation
1968	Pilgrim Baptist Church, Outstanding Roanoke Citizen
1968	Sun Oil Company, Outstanding Roanoke Citizen
1968 & 1969	Virginia Jaycees, Outstanding State Chairman
1969	"Key Man" for work with retarded children, highest award of Virginia Jaycees (award not given in previous five years)
1969	Virginia Association for Retarded Children, Certificate of Award
1969	North Carolina Mutual Life Insurance Company, "Mr. Achiever"
1969	United State Jaycees, Outstanding Mental Retardation Chairman in United States
1969	Omega Psi Phi Fraternity, Citizen of the Year
1970	Roanoke Area Association for Retarded Children, Distinguished Service Award
1970	Harrison School, Outstanding Citizen Award for work with schoolchildren
1971	"Bill Robertson Day" held in Roanoke, Virginia, Distinguished Achievement Plaque
1971	Main Building at Camp Virginia Jaycee designated "Robertson Hall"
1972	National Conference of Christians and Jews, Annual Certificate Award for dedication to the principles and ideals of the Brotherhood of Man
1972	Honorary doctorate from Virginia College, Lynchburg
1973	National Business League, J. C. Napier Government Man of the Year Award for qualities of leadership in the interest of minority business enterprise
1973	William B. Robertson Community Service Award is a national award given annually at the United States Jaycees Convention.

It is presented to the Jaycee chapter in this country with the most outstanding project geared toward providing a better quality of life for the people of that particular community. He was one of the few living persons and the only African American to have a national Jaycee award named in his honor.

1973	President's Committee on Mental Retardation, Certificate Citation for Camp Virginia Jaycee
1976	National Education Association, State Winner from Virginia of NEA Special Bicentennial Award
1977	Peace Corps, Certificate of Superior Achievement
1979	Family of Jomo Kenyatta, Plaque, Outstanding Service to the Republic of Kenya
1979	Kenya Jaycees, Kenya (JCI) Distinguished Service Award
1986	Honorary doctorate, Southeastern University, Washington, D.C.
1987	United States Jaycees Hall of Fame
1990	Citizen of the Year, Reston, Virginia
2006	Finalist, Teacher of the Year, Hillsborough County, Florida, "We Deliver" award to honor teachers who "deliver miracles every day"
2007	Roanoke College's Margaret Sue Copenhaver Contributions to Education Award for advocacy of mental retardation awareness.
2019	Renaming of the Bluefield State College Library to the "William B. Robertson Library"

BIBLIOGRAPHY

"Aide to Former Gov. Holton to Head Peace Corps in Kenya." *Danville Register,* December 1975, 14. William B. Robertson Papers, Archives Collection, Bluefield State College.

Allen, Elizabeth Jones. "Helping the Handicapped: A Partnership with Kenya." *Topic Magazine,* no. 168 (1984): 50–55. William B. Robertson Papers, Archives Collection, Bluefield State College.

"Apartheid." History.com, May 6, 2019. www.history.com/topics/africa/apartheid.

Archer, Bill. "Stroke of Luck Let Robertson Break Color Barriers in Time of Segregation." *Bluefield Daily Telegraph,* February 10, 2007, 1.

Armstrong, Sue. "Forum: Watching the Race Detectives—The Results of South African Race Classification Laws." *New Scientist,* April 20, 1991. www .newscientist.com/article/mg13017656–200-forum-watching-the-race -detectives-the-results-of-south-africas-race-classification-laws/.

Atkin, Jerry. "Roanoke's Robertson Honored." *Roanoke Times,* March 30, 1971. William B. Robertson Papers, Archives Collection, Bluefield State College.

Barnes, Catherine. "Incentives, Sanctions, and Conditionality." *Accord* 19 (February 2008). http://www.c-r.org/accord/incentives-sanctions-and-conditionality /international-isolation-and-pressure-change-south.

Barnes, Lottie Rebecca. Obituary. *Baltimore Sun,* December 16, 1980, 42.

Bayer, Richard C. "Holton Aide Defends Black Trooper Policy." *Norfolk Ledger-Star,* January 26, 1972.

Bluefield State College Official Channel. Video file: "Bluefield State College Robertson Library Rededication." January 29, 2020. www.youtube.com/watch?v =LzuNS2JX-rQ.

Boddy-Evans, Alistair. "16 June 1976 Student Uprising in Soweto." *Thought Co.,* July 3, 2019. www.thoughtco.com/student-uprising-soweto-riots-part -1–43425.

Brown, Marilyn. "Giving Back a Lifetime." *Tampa Tribune,* April 11, 2005, 1. William B. Robertson Papers, Archives Collection, Bluefield State College.

Carico, Melville. "City GOP Nominates Butler, Robertson." *Roanoke Times,* June 6, 1969. William B. Robertson Papers, Archives Collection, Bluefield State College.

Casey, Dan. "Casey: Deal Appears Near to Sell Camp Virginia Jaycee." *Roanoke Times,* October 8, 2018. www.roanoke.com/news/local/casey-deal -appears-near-to-sell-camp-virginia-jaycee/article_3be4b91f-58d9–5279 -b220–78def9b2b96c.html.

"Citizen of the Year: Robertson, Heart for People." *Reston Times,* January 3, 1990, A-1–3. William B. Robertson Papers, Archives Collection, Bluefield State College.

Coleman, Max, ed. "A Crime Against Humanity." Human Rights Committee of South Africa, 1998. https://sahistory.org.za/archive/detention-weapon.

"Cooling-Off Period Set at Prison." *Staunton News Leader,* December 18, 1972. William B. Robertson Papers, Archives Collection, Bluefield State College.

Dellinger, Paul. "Mental Patient Takes Hostage." *Roanoke Times,* June 30, 1970. William B. Robertson Papers, Archives Collection, Bluefield State College.

Dewar, Helen. "Negro Is Named as Aide to Holton." *Washington Post,* January 14, 1970, C1. William B. Robertson Papers, Archives Collection, Bluefield State College.

Duff, Jim. "Robertson Gives $10,000 to Camp for Retarded Kids." *Richmond Afro-American,* March 15, 1975. William B. Robertson Papers, Archives Collection, Bluefield State College.

Edwards, Robin. "Big Blue Alumni Gather to Save Black Colleges." *Roanoke Times and World-News,* July 29, 1984, B-7. William B. Robertson Papers, Archives Collection, Bluefield State College.

Ellis, Rebecca. "Annoyed Baltimore Drivers Want City to Crack Down on Squeegee Kids." *NPR News,* December 9, 2018. www.npr.org/2018/12/09/667155718 /annoyed-baltimore-drivers-want-city-to-crack-down-on-squeegee-kids.

Farrar, Wayne. "Holton Names Roanoke Negro as Aide." *Roanoke Times,* January 14, 1970. William B. Robertson Papers, Archives Collection, Bluefield State College.

——. "Patient with Hostage Wanted to See Robertson." *Roanoke Times,* July 1, 1970. William B. Robertson Papers, Archives Collection, Bluefield State College.

"Film Depicts Roanoke's Work with Retarded Youth." *Roanoke World-News,* June 22, 1968, 7. William B. Robertson Papers, Archives Collection, Bluefield State College.

George, Justin. "Handing Down History, Handing Down Dreams." *Tampa Bay Times,* March 23, 2012, 1. William B. Robertson Papers, Archives Collection, Bluefield State College.

Gill, Laverne. *Reston's African American Legacy.* Vol. 1. Akron, OH: 48 Hour Books, 2017.

Griisser, Gayle. "Care for Retarded Spans Continent." *The News* (Lynchburg, VA), July 13, 1983, B1–2. William B. Robertson Papers, Archives Collection, Bluefield State College.

"Hanover School First for Textbooks." *Daily Dispatch* (East London, South Africa), October 27, 1994. William B. Robertson Papers, Archives Collection, Bluefield State College.

"Harris, Robertson Hit Biased Books." *Afro-American,* August 21, 1970. William B. Robertson Papers, Archives Collection, Bluefield State College.

Hayes, Gwendolyn. "Sligh Teacher Assists in Presenting National Award Named in His Honor." *Florida Sentinel Bulletin,* March 26, 2004. William B. Robertson Papers, Archives Collection, Bluefield State College.

Hillsborough County Schools. "We Deliver Miracles Every Day." Collection of Nominations from 2011. Tampa, Florida.

"History of Apartheid in South Africa." South Africa History Online, May 6, 2016. www.sahistory.org.za/article/history-apartheid-south-africa.

Holton, Linwood. *Opportunity Time.* Charlottesville: University of Virginia Press, 2008.

Hoy, Bill. "Kenyans Use Camp Jaycee as Learning Experience." *Bedford Bulletin Democrat,* July 6, 1983. William B. Robertson Papers, Archives Collection, Bluefield State College.

"Jaycees' Key Award Revived for Roanoker." *Roanoke World-News,* May 19, 1969. William B. Robertson Papers, Archives Collection, Bluefield State College.

Kapuściński, Ryszard. *The Cobra's Heart.* London: Penguin, 2007.

Kimathi, Joe. "Nyeri, Reston: 'Twins' Who Work Together." *Sunday Nation* (Nairobi, Kenya), December 9, 1984. William B. Robertson Papers, Archives Collection, Bluefield State College.

Lanyi, Nikolas. "Kenyan Thanks Restonians for Medical Education." *Reston Connection,* January 12, 1994, 8. William B. Robertson Papers, Archives Collection, Bluefield State College.

Lentczner, Joan T. "Bill Robertson: No Turning Back." *Radford University Magazine,* February 1984, 24–27. William B. Robertson Papers, Archives Collection, Bluefield State College.

Lucy Addison High School Yearbook. 1950. www.virginiaroom.org/digital/files /original/17/2738/The_Addisonian_1950.pdf.

Mahoney, Rachel. "Crisis Response Non-Profit Sets up Camp at Old Jaycee Grounds." *Lynchburg News & Advance,* April 7, 2019. www.newsadvance.com /news/local/crisis-response-nonprofit-sets-up-camp-at-old-jaycee-grounds /article_c8796ef7-08d7-5372-a644-e040be044966.html.

Mascarenas, Isabel. "Mister Robertson: A Statesman and a Teacher." *Tampa Bay Times,* September 10, 2008. www.tampabays10.com/includes/tools/print.aspx ?storyid=91765.

"Match Maker Fair, A Great Success." *Witwatersrand Chamber of Commerce & Industry Bulletin,* June 13, 1988.

"Member of Holton Staff Joins Nixon Staff in Capital." *Danville Register,* July 18, 1973, 3. William B. Robertson Papers, Archives Collection, Bluefield State College.

Menya, M. J., to Caspar Weinberger. November 26, 1982. William B. Robertson Papers, Archives Collection, Bluefield State College.

Miller, Kevin, ed. "The Heart of Apartheid." *BBC News,* September 10, 1968. www.bbc.co.uk/worldserviceradio.

Ndlovu, Sifiso Mxolisi. "The Soweto Uprising." In *The Road to Democracy in South Africa* (PDF), vol. 2, p. 344. South African Democracy Education Trust. www.sadet.co.za/docs/RTD/vol2/Volume%202%20-%20chapter%207.pdf.

Nelson, Jim. "BSC Library Renamed to Honor Alumnus William B. Robertson." https://bluefieldstate.edu/community/news-and-events/bsc-library-renamed-honor-alumnus-william-b-robertson.

"Not Just Another 'Think' Conference." *Roanoke World-News,* October 22, 1971.

Novak, Rebecca. "Vice President's Spouse Praises Bedford Camp for Mentally Retarded." July 6, 1988, *Bedford (VA) Bulletin,* 1 and 8. William B. Robertson Papers, Archives Collection, Bluefield State College.

Nuckols, Christina. "Crusading with Confidence: Linwood Holton 30 Years Later." *Roanoke Times,* September 5, 1999. William B. Robertson Papers, Archives Collection, Bluefield State College.

——. "Former Governors Toast Camp Founder." *Roanoke Times,* October 16, 1999. William B. Robertson Papers, Archives Collection, Bluefield State College.

"Nyeri Students Reflect." *Reston Times,* September 9, 1987. William B. Robertson Papers, Archives Collection, Bluefield State College.

"115 Joy-Filled Newsies Return Home from N.Y.C." *Afro-American,* October 8, 1956. William B. Robertson Papers, Archives Collection, Bluefield State College.

Pancake, John. "Danes Impress Visiting Virginia Girl." *Roanoke World-News,* November 4, 1971, 32. William B. Robertson Papers, Archives Collection, Bluefield State College.

——. "Robertson Encouraged by Recruiting Efforts." *Roanoke World-News,* December 2, 1971, 33. William B. Robertson Papers, Archives Collection, Bluefield State College.

Pearson, Michael, and Tom Cohen. "Life under Apartheid: Demeaning, Often Brutal." *CNN,* December 6, 2013. www.cnn.com/2013/12/06/world/africa/mandela-life-under-apartheid/index.html.

Poff, Mag. "Bill Robertson: Years of Segregation Best Forgotten." *Roanoke Times and World News,* April 4, 1984, A11. William B. Robertson Papers, Archives Collection, Bluefield State College.

———. "Former Roanoker Plans to Aid Black Firms in S. Africa." *Roanoke Times and World-News,* October 7, 1986. William B. Robertson Papers, Archives Collection, Bluefield State College.

———. "Minority Conference Becomes a Story of Success." *Roanoke Times and World News,* October 8, 1981, B1 and 4. William B. Robertson Papers, Archives Collection, Bluefield State College.

———. "Roanokers Find the Full Life in Kenya." *Roanoke Times and World-News,* December 25, 1977, E-2. William B. Robertson Papers, Archives Collection, Bluefield State College.

Pruitt, Sarah. "How Emmett Till's Murder Galvanized the Civil Rights Movement." November 2018. www.history.com/news/new-book-sheds-light-on-the-murder-of-emmett-till-the-civil-rights-movement.

Reed, Betty. "Kenyan Teachers Visit Reston." *Reston Times,* August 11, 1983. William B. Robertson Papers, Archives Collection, Bluefield State College.

"Roanoke Native Receives Margaret Sue Copenhaver Contribution to Education Award." *Roanoke Tribune,* July 5, 2007, 1. William B. Robertson Papers, Archives Collection, Bluefield State College.

Robertson, Jackie Frank. Obituary. *Daily World,* September 20, 1999, 4.

Robertson, Patrick G. Obituary. February 2017. www.legacy.com/obituaries/name/patrick-robertson-obituary?pid=183983964.

Robertson, Vincent. Obituary. March 2007. https://wrightmortuary.com/tribute/details/1233/Vincent-Robertson/obituary.html.

Robertson, William B. Address. Hugh O'Brian Youth Foundation Alumni Association, Virginia Chapter Reunion, Fredericksburg, August 22, 1987. William B. Robertson Papers, Archives Collection, Bluefield State College.

———. Address. Sister Cities International Conference, Worthington Hotel, Fort Worth, TX, July 17, 1987. William B. Robertson Papers, Archives Collection, Bluefield State College.

———. "America's Role in Africa—The Importance of U.S. Commercial and Investment Presence in the Context of U.S. Foreign Policy." Trade and Investment Conference on Africa, Miami, FL, April 16, 1986. William B. Robertson Papers, Archives Collection, Bluefield State College.

———. Commencement Address. Bluefield State College, May 2019. William B. Robertson Papers, Archives Collection, Bluefield State College.

———. Interview by Peggy Turnbull. No date [1981?]. William B. Robertson Papers, Archives Collection, Bluefield State College.

———. "Like Colin Kaepernick, We Should All Take a Knee." *Baltimore Sun,* September 7, 2017. www.baltimoresun.com/opinion/readers-respond/bs-ed-rr-kaepernick-20170907-story.html.

———. Memo to Secretary of Defense. December 13, 1982. Typescript. William B. Robertson Papers, Archives Collection, Bluefield State College.

———. Remarks. Bluefield State Foundation, Inc., Elks Country Club, Bluefield, WV, November 20, 2004. William B. Robertson Papers, Archives Collection, Bluefield State College.

———. "Robertson: Happy Jackie Robinson Day." *Roanoke Times,* April 12, 2009. www.roanoke.com/opinion/commentary/robertson-happy-jackie-robinson -day/article_e42cde66-dbb6-520b-8424-3736e0570a8f.html.

———. "Symposium on Apartheid and the United States." East Carolina University, Greenville, NC, March 25, 1986. William B. Robertson Papers, Archives Collection, Bluefield State College.

———. "U.S. Wants an End to Apartheid." United States Department of State, Bureau of Public Affairs, Current Policy No. 787. January 18, 1986. William B. Robertson Papers, Archives Collection, Bluefield State College.

———. "Woody's Job Corps: A 1973 Lesson for 'Squeegee Kids' and Baltimore as a Whole." *Baltimore Sun,* October 25, 2019. www.baltimoresun.com/opinion/op -ed/bs-ed-op-1027-woody-job-corps-20191025-k5ubwzmhpnbrff6syblgqx4wt4 -story.html.

Robertson, William B., and Barbara Starling Ricks. "Development Proposal to Ghana from CHEER, Inc." September 1995. William B. Robertson Papers, Archives Collection, Bluefield State College.

"Robertson: Citizen of the Year." *Reston Times,* n.d., 1989, A1. William B. Robertson Papers, Archives Collection, Bluefield State College.

"Robertson First Negro Appointed to Executive Staff of a Virginia Governor." *Roanoke Tribune,* January 15, 1970. William B. Robertson Papers, Archives Collection, Bluefield State College.

"Robertson Honored by National Jaycees." *Reston Times,* January 3, 1988. William B. Robertson Papers, Archives Collection, Bluefield State College.

"Robertson Picked for Safety Panel." *Richmond Afro-American,* January 22, 1972. William B. Robertson Papers, Archives Collection, Bluefield State College.

"Robertson Splitting Time between Richmond and Tech." *Roanoke Times,* Montgomery edition, October 2, 1973, M1. William B. Robertson Papers, Archives Collection, Bluefield State College.

Robinson, David. *The Conversation,* October 10, 2018. http://theconversation.com /world-politics-explainer-the-end-of-apartheid-101602. William B. Robertson Papers, Archives Collection, Bluefield State College.

"South's State Patrol Units Still Have Very Few Blacks." *Atlanta Journal,* January 31, 1972. William B. Robertson Papers, Archives Collection, Bluefield State College.

"State Funds Requested for Spanish-Speaking." *Richmond Times-Dispatch,* September 12, 1970. William B. Robertson Papers, Archives Collection, Bluefield State College.

Taylor, Cissy. "There Can Only Be Americans." *Petersburg Progress-Index,* Sep-

tember 23, 1971, 1. William B. Robertson Papers, Archives Collection, Bluefield
State College.

"Teddy Roosevelt's Shocking Dinner with Washington." *NPR News,* May 14, 2012.
www.npr.org/2012/05/14/152684575/teddy-roosevelts-shocking-dinner-with
-washington.

Tunnell, Harry. *The Negro Motorist Green Book 1936–1964.* July 29, 2014. www
.Blackpast.org/african-american-history/negro-motorist-green-book-1936
-1964/.

"U.S. Official Visits Ghana." *Xinhua Overseas News Service,* May 10, 1987. William B. Robertson Papers, Archives Collection, Bluefield State College.

"Wanted: More Black State Troopers." *Roanoke World-News,* May 26, 1970. William B. Robertson Papers, Archives Collection, Bluefield State College.

"William B. Robertson Living by Example." *Jaycees Magazine* 2, no. 4 (August/
September 1988): 27–29. William B. Robertson Papers, Archives Collection,
Bluefield State College.

"William Robertson Appointed to National Retardation Unit." *World-News,*
July 17, 1970. William B. Robertson Papers, Archives Collection, Bluefield State
College.

"William Robertson from Afro Paperboy to Four-Time Presidential Appointee."
Afro-American, September 9, 2016. www.afro.com/from=afro=paperboy-to-4
-time-presidential-appointee/#.

Wooldridge, Mike. "World Still Learning from Ethiopia Famine." *BBC News,*
November 2014. www.bbc.com/news/world-africa-30211448.

INDEX

President's Committee on Mental Retardation, 42, 70, 111, 115, 161, 179
Pretoria, South Africa, 123, 166
Prince Edward County, Virginia, 55, 58
Puerto Ricans, 162
Pulaski, Virginia, 60

Radford, Virginia, 39–40, 55
Radford College (University), Radford, Virginia, 39, 40, 151, 177
Railway Express Company, 13, 17, 23–24
Rankin, John R., 8
Ray, Robert, 94–95
Reagan, Maureen, 118
Reagan, Ronald, 115–16, 118, 120, 123, 125–26, 169–71
Reston, Virginia, 109–13, 115, 179
Rhodes, Cecil, 123
Rhodesia/Zimbabwe, 123
Richmond, Virginia: apple jelly sales, 47, 54; family in, 113, 140; governor's office in, 69, 92, 100; Holton inauguration in, 57; jobs in, 60, 62, 76, 86; NAACP in, 90; VPI half-time while in, 93–94; Woody's Job Corps, 88, 153
Richmond Community Action Program, 88
Richmond Times, 57, 196
Richmond Urban League, 88
Ricks, Barbara, 129–30
Ritchie, Jeanne, 64
Roanoke, Virginia: Camp Virginia Jaycee in, 144–45, 176; childhood in, 1–2, 12, 150–51; and college, 5–6, 9–10; culture of, 15–18; family in, 138–41; integration in, 50; Jayees in, 41–43, 47–48; jobs in, 62; media in, 23, 50, 57, 71, 100–101; moving

from, 69; politics of, 51–55; problem-solving in, 75; recognition by, 73, 177–79; recreation in, 44–45, 18–19; romance while living in, 131; schools in, 19, 28, 35–37, 39, 130; segregation in, 51; sister cities of, 107, 110; teaching while in, 31–33; Elsie Wiggins, fellow student from, 40
Roanoke Area Association for Retarded Children, 42, 178
Roanoke City Council, 43, 51, 53
Roanoke City Democratic Party, 52
Roanoke City Recreation Department, 43
Roanoke City Young Democrats, 52
Roanoke College, Roanoke, Virginia, 6, 43, 179
Roanoke Fine Arts Center, 43
Roanoke Tribune, 23, 51
Roberts, Mary (maternal grandmother of WBR), 13
Roberts, William (maternal grandfather of WBR), 13
Robertson, Allen. *See* Robertson, William Allen
Robertson, Barry (brother of WBR), 12, 138
Robertson, Cynthia Powell (daughter-in-law of WBR), 141
Robertson, Ellen Marie (sister of WBR), 12, 139
Robertson, Eva Marie (granddaughter of WBR), 141
Robertson, Faye (sister of WBR), 12–13, 16, 21, 130
Robertson, Irvin (father of WBR), 12
Robertson, Jackie Frank Lewis (brother of WBR), 12, 26, 130
Robertson, Nora (paternal grandmother of WBR), 14

Robertson, Patrick (brother of WBR), 12, 139

Robertson, Ruth Price (wife of WBR), 9, 15–16, 21, 130, 132

Robertson, Stanley (brother of WBR), 12, 13, 23, 26, 75

Robertson, Teddy Allen (grandson of WBR), 141

Robertson, Victoria (daughter of WBR): childhood of, 35–39, 139–41; at college, 93, 100; in Denmark, 71; experience as daughter of WBR, 139; in high school, 69, 71, 140; in Kenya, 102, 105–6; learns about segregation through Lakeside commercial, 50; and meditation, 140–41; and Peace Corps, 140; understanding of disabilities, 47

Robertson, Vincent (brother of WBR), 12

Robertson, William (paternal grandfather of WBR), 14

Robertson, William Allen (Allen, son of WCR): as infant, 36–39; in Kenya, 105; and music, 105, 141; in parade, 46–47; schools attended, 69, 71, 93, 100, 141; experience as son of WBR, 139; speaking with Governor Godwin, 54–55

Robertson, William Bernard: call to action of, 148–54; and Camp Virginia Jaycee, 46–48, 142–45; childhood of, 12–28; college years of, 5–11, 30; family of, 12, 138–41; and Jaycees, 41–46; in Kenya, 99–114; marriages of, 10, 124; at State Department, 115–26; teaching, 31–34, 132–37; in Virginia governor's office, 57–89; at Virginia Polytechnic Institute, 92–99

Robertson, Zelmer Batemon (sister-in-law of WBR), 130

Robinson, Jackie, 24–26

Roosevelt, Teddy, 159

Salem, Peter, 157

Salomon, Norbert, 106

San Juan Hill, 159

segregation: in baseball, 25, 35; Governor Byrd and, 55; at colleges, 11, 37, 51; current, 149, 153, 165; evils of, 1, 16–17, 27; family as victims of, 50; and Jaycees, 42, 161; and jobs, 60; Robert Kennedy advocating against, 49; in Roanoke, 6, 15, 150; in schools, 19, 23, 32, 58, 140; South African apartheid compared to, 122, 126; travel and, 6, 17, 23, 32; in U.S. history, 17, 73, 137, 174; U.S. Supreme Court ends, in public schools, 11; in Virginia, 55, 87

Seven Years' War, 156

Seychelles, 106, 140

Shelton, Catherine, 96

Shriver, Eunice Kennedy, 107

Shriver, Sargent, 107

Shultz, George P., 115–16, 126

Siena Heights College, Ohio, 139

Sierra Leone, 111

Sister Cities, 110–12, 121, 126–27, 129

slavery: in African history, 106, 122; dance created by enslaved people, 106; evils of, 1, 149–50, 150, 156; myths about, 72–73; overcoming, 19, 159, 173–74; in U.S. history, 14, 19, 122, 166

Slayton, Addison, 77, 79, 82

Sligh Middle School, Tampa, Florida, 132–35

Small Business Administration, 61–62

Smith, A. Byron, 51

South Africa: apartheid in, 116, 119, 122–26, 165–74; books donated to, 128–29, 144; jobs in, 121; penguins in, 117; teacher exchange with, 111, 128–29

Southeastern University, Washington, D.C., 179

Southwestern State Hospital, Marion, Virginia, 63–64, 66

Southwest Virginia Veterans Cemetery, Dublin, Virginia, 139

Spanish-American War, 159

squeegee boys, 149

State Department, 115–16, 118, 126, 129, 173

St. Francis de Sales, Powhatan, Virginia, 139

St. Paul's College, Lawrenceville, Virginia, 6, 112

St. Peter Claver Church, Tampa, Florida, 151

St. Thomas a Becket Catholic Church, Reston, Virginia, 112

Sullivan, Rev. Leon, 168

Sullivan principles, 168

Swahili, 101, 105, 117

Tambo, Oliver, 171

Taylor, Noel C., 53

textbooks, failings of, 72–73, 157

Thomas, Chaplain Walter, 77

Thomas, Christie, 144, 176

Tidewater Association for Retarded Children, Virginia, 74

Till, Emmett, 90–91

Tilson, Arthur, 65

Toliaferro, Wadine Henrietta (niece of WBR), 130

Towe, Darden, 44, 54

Transkei, Africa, 128

Treeside School, Nairobi, 105, 107

Tribune (Roanoke, Virginia), 57

Trump, Donald J., 55, 143, 150

Tubman, Harriet, 73

Tucker, Sam, 90

Tunnell, Harry, 32

Tuskegee Airmen, 22

Tutu, Bishop Desmond, 164–65

Twenty-Fourth Infantry Division, 160

Underwood, Juanita, 133

University of Virginia, Charlottesville, 6, 190

Vickers, Angela, 135

Vietnam, 155, 160

Vipassana meditation, 140

Virginia Association for Retarded Citizens, 44, 70, 178

Virginia Beach, Virginia, 47

Virginia Commonwealth University, Richmond, 113, 141

Virginia Department of Human Resources, 75

Virginia House of Delegates, 53–54

Virginia Mental Health Institute, 66

Virginia Polytechnic Institute and State University (Virginia Tech, VPI), 6, 39, 92–93, 96, 105, 140

Virginia Seminary, Lynchburg, 28

Virginia State Alcoholic Beverage Control (ABC) Board, 60

Virginia State College, Petersburg, 28, 39, 40

Virginia State Penitentiary, Richmond, 77, 83

Virginia State Police, 59, 65–66, 85

voting, 52–53, 58, 125, 173–74

Wampler, William, 55

Wanyama, Patrick, 112